healthy eating during
chemotherapy

José van Mil with
Christine Archer-Mackenzie

healthy eating during
chemotherapy

For the first time, a chef and a medical specialist have
teamed up to inspire you with over 100 delicious recipes

Photography by Henk Brandsen
Kyle Books

An Hachette UK Company
www.hachette.co.uk

First published in Great Britain in 2008 by
Kyle Books, an imprint of Kyle Cathie Ltd
Carmelite House
50 Victoria Embankment
London EC4Y 0DZ
www.kylebooks.co.uk

ISBN 978 0 85783 793 6

Project Editor: Suzanna de Jong
Design: pinkstripedesign@hotmail.com
Copy Editor: Anna Hitchin
Proofreader: Lesley Levene
Editorial Assistant: Vicki Murrell
Indexer: Alex Corrin
Photographer: Henk Brandsen
Home Economists: José van Mil, Hanneke Boers and Nadia Zerouali
Prop Stylist: Jan Willem van Riel
Production: Sha Huxtable

A Cataloguing in Publication record for this title is available from the British Library.

Printed and bound in China

10 9 8 7 6 5 4 3 2 1

contents

a world to thank

Having a dream is one thing, but to accomplish it, is quite a different matter. It's just like real life, you need the support, enthusiasm, encouragement, inspiration and professional knowledge and feed back from others. And my goodness, what a beautiful bunch of people I have had to support me. Dr. Christine (Chrissie) Archer-Mackenzie who has spend so much time and energy to provide a sound medical, nutritional and cancer related base. Marja Lantinga, dietitian at VUMC, who advised me on what patients can and won't eat and many other things related to food and cancer. Then inevitably my husband, writer Paul Somberg, who unfortunately was both patient and at times 'ghost writer' and my dear friend Ruth Archer who read, reread and rereread the manuscript and kept me sharp. As did Olga van Itallie, Lia Brouwer, Carla van Mil and Katinka Paul.

Any book is a team effort. I may have written it, but this book is far more than words and recipes. The photo team did a magnificent job in picturing the dishes as attractively and realistically as possible. What a great job you made of it, Henk, Jan Willem, Hanneke and Nadia; thank you ever so much for your professionalism and support.

All the recipes have obviously been tested extensively. Firstly in my trial kitchen (thank you Jasper and again Nadia) and then by many others who found themselves in difficulties with food related problems due to their treatment. It was under these extremely difficult conditions that they crossed borders and tried the recipes. Thanks a lot Paul, Jorien, Ron, Reina and all the others who – however ill – rewardingly confirmed that my approach to food for patients undergoing radiation and chemotherapy had an uplifting effect on them.

You can write a book, but getting it publicised is another matter. Thank you Kyle Cathie, Suzanna de Jong (my reliable and very professional guide), Anna Hitchin, Lesley Levene, Mark Latter, Inmerc's John Voskens (who believed in the concept from the onset), Chris van Koppen (you're great) and last but not least Frits Poiesz, a magnificent partner who straightened whatever ripples were left.

Finely I owe a lot to my grandma 'Oma Dien' who gave me the first insight in the value of certain foods when you're ill. She took me blackberry picking to make juice to help to cure my sister's measles. It worked.

you are my source of inspiration

To write this cookery book I have found my inspiration in my fantastic husband Paul, but also in Ian, Mignon, Ron and all those others – patients and their supporters – whom all of a sudden find themselves confronted with food related problems due to chemo and radiation treatments.

To Paul and all these others I dedicate this book and hope they can find some joy and pleasure by eating and drinking well and manage to keep up their strength.

José van Mil

introduction

a harsh reality

All of a sudden the penny dropped – there was something terribly wrong with my husband. Not just a common cold, not a backache, nor a spell of tiredness. No, it was something much more serious. The word sent shivers up my spine: cancer.

Immediate and radical treatments were required to bring things under control. Fortunately, the medical profession has come a long way in the treatment of cancer and the prospects for recovery are improving each year. In my husband's case, chemotherapy and radiotherapy were amongst the things in store for him. In order to successfully pass through this ordeal, it was crucial to make sure that he would not lose weight through malnourishment or lack of appetite. Normally he loves his food but the effects of the treatment took their toll. Eating became a huge burden. And he was not alone in that. I talked to numerous cancer patients, their relatives and friends and almost all of them had encountered eating problems.

I therefore decided to make the most of my professional experience as a chef to develop a method to make eating easier for him. I contacted Christine Archer-Mackenzie who improved my method and made valuable contributions from a medical point of view. Marja Lantinga, an oncological dietitian, advised me on what patients can and will not eat and provided insight in many other aspects to do with food and cancer. The method worked; all the way through radiotherapy, intense chemotherapy and stem cell transplantation, my husband lost hardly any weight. Remarkably soon afterwards, he regained his strength and had fully recovered his appetite. Since then, other patients have tried my method – it inspired most of them to keep eating and provided me with useful feedback.

I am not offering you a miracle cure but, hopefully, this book will help cancer patients to keep eating and, by doing so, aid recovery from their treatment. It's definitely worth trying.

And through it all, be strong and keep up your spirits.
José van Mil

cancer and food

what is cancer?

Cells are constantly being replaced in the body. Each area of our body has a specialised function and specialised cells to perform that function. The way cells multiply is by dividing to create an exact replica with the same hereditary information (DNA). Normally cell division is controlled so that a relatively constant size is maintained throughout adult life. Sometimes a fault can occur which causes cells to divide more rapidly than they should. A mechanism is in place to control this, but if this also fails the cell replication rate of these 'faulty' cells accelerates. The faulty cells absorb more nutrients and thus divide at an ever-increasing rate to form a tumour. If these cells remain self-contained and do not leave their specific area, they are known as benign or non-cancerous cells. If the cells have the ability to invade neighbouring tissue, they are then called cancer cells and produce cancerous tumours. When cancer cells invade other parts of the body, this is referred to as metastasis.

treatments for cancer

SURGERY

Surgery is the oldest form of treatment. It can be used both to diagnose and to treat cancer. It may be the sole treatment necessary or it may not be used at all, depending on the site and the kind of cancer. Sometimes it is supplemented with other treatments, such as chemotherapy and radiotherapy.

CHEMOTHERAPY

Chemotherapy (and also radiotherapy) works by preventing cancer cells from multiplying. This is achieved by interfering with the cells' DNA so they are unable to replicate. The treatment can also cause some cancer cells to commit suicide. Chemotherapy involves having anti-cancer drugs administered into the bloodstream so that the whole body is affected. It's a powerful treatment that kills cancer cells and healthy cells alike. During chemotherapy, the body is not only fighting cancer but, at the same time, replacing healthy cells that are damaged by the chemotherapy drugs. Chemotherapy and radiotherapy particularly affect the cells lining the digestive tract, hair follicles and bone marrow, resulting in problems with the mouth and throat, hair loss, anaemia, bleeding and an inability to fight infection.

SIDE EFFECTS

Common side effects during chemotherapy are changes in the sense of smell and taste, nausea, vomiting, mouth sores, anaemia, changes in bowel habits, fatigue, pain and weight loss. The general overall effect for patients is a combination of tiredness and lethargy, which in turn can lead to lack of appetite.

the importance of food

For people undergoing cancer treatment food becomes very important. They require good nutritional support to maintain body weight and strength, to prevent body tissue from breaking down, to rebuild tissue, and to fight infection and fatigue. At the same time, the side effects of treatment often have a significant impact on the consumption of food and eating habits. They can affect the absorption and digestion of food, creating a health risk for cancer sufferers. Therefore, nutritional care is needed to maximise quality of life.

Scientific studies have now proved that good nutritional support helps the appetite, decreases the toxicity that is associated with treatment and can alleviate side effects, all of which significantly improve patients' survival rates.

The idea that food is good for one's health is not new. More than 4,000 years ago, both the ancient Egyptians and the ancient Greeks used honey medicinally for burns, sores and wounds. Hippocrates (460–377 BC) believed in the benefits of good food – 'Let food be thy medicine and medicine be thy food' – and emphasised the importance of using fresh plants and herbs in his diet.

WHY ARE CERTAIN FOODS SO IMPORTANT IN THE DIET OF CANCER PATIENTS?

In the 1990s, phytochemical compounds were discovered in fruit and vegetables. These are plant-specific compounds that protect the plants from disease, oxidation, insect infestation and radiation. When we eat these compounds – called phytonutrients – they have a similar protective effect on our bodies. Phytonutrients can have anti-inflammatory, anti-bacterial and anti-cancer properties in humans. The American National Cancer Institute is currently involved in research looking at the importance of these phytochemicals in cancer prevention and cancer treatments.

It will take scientists many more years before they know exactly how phytochemicals work. Following are some examples of foods containing phytonutrients that show promising results when it comes to fighting cancer.

ANTIOXIDANTS

To understand the importance of antioxidants, first we need to talk about free radicals. Oxygen is utilised by cells in our bodies – it is fundamental to our most basic mechanisms. Free radicals are the natural by-product of the oxidation process. These free radicals travel through cells, causing damage to the DNA and cell membranes. This damage can encourage the development of cancer in the cells.

Antioxidants work to prevent cells from becoming cancerous by enabling early cancer cells to become healthy again. Antioxidants can also prevent cancer by decreasing the levels of free radicals in the body.

You can compare the workings of free radicals and antioxidants with what happens to an avocado when you cut it open and expose the flesh. The avocado will turn brown due to oxidation which releases free radicals. If you squeeze some lemon juice over the avocado, the juice, acting as an antioxidant, stops the avocado from browning.

A number of foods contain antioxidants with the potential to support cancer treatments. Their strength can vary enormously. Examples of antioxidants and foods containing high levels of antioxidants are:

Phenols – found in berries, grapes, mustard, olive oil, sesame seeds and tea.

Selenium – a strong antioxidant that works best in combination with vitamin E, it's found in avocados, brazil nuts, brewer's yeast, cereals, grains, shellfish and sunflower seeds.

Vitamin E – occurs in avocados, egg yolks, nuts, olive oil, seeds, tuna and wheat germ.

Beta carotene – found in brightly coloured fruit and vegetables, especially those containing yellow pigment; functions as an antioxidant that can prevent cancer; good sources are apricots, beetroot, broccoli, cantaloupe melons, carrots, cherries, peaches, peppers, pumpkins, spinach, squashes and sweet potatoes.

Vitamin C – noted for its high antioxidant activity, it has a protective effect on normal cells and a sensitising effect on cancer cells; good sources are blackcurrants, citrus fruits, parsley, rosehips and all fruit and vegetables containing vitamin C.

Biflavenoids – these pigments, found in fruit and vegetables, stop or slow the growth of cancer cells; good sources are apricots, lemons and melons. Bioflavonoids and vitamin C are found in many of the same foods and together, they seem to have a positive effect on the immune system, which is very important when chemotherapy compromises the immune system. Foods that contain both vitamin C and bioflavonoids include the skins of grapes and the peel and pith of citrus fruits.

Also high in antioxidants are green tea, lycopene (found in cooked tomatoes), pomegranate juice and artichokes, while curcumin (turmeric) acts as an antioxidant in normal cells and can cause cancer cells to die.

OTHER BENEFICIAL PHYTONUTRIENTS AND FOODS

Shiitake mushrooms contain a compound called **lentinan** which is believed to stop or slow tumour growth and have a positive effect on the immune system. In Japan, lentinan is given to patients undergoing chemotherapy for lung, nose, throat and stomach cancers.

Current research suggests a potential benefit from the use of **phyto-oestrogens**, especially in hormone-related cancers such as breast and prostate. They are effective in blocking cancer-promoting oestrogens and they also reduce the toxic effect of chemotherapy and radiotherapy. Phyto-oestrogens are found in linseed, rhubarb and soya.

A substance called **IP6**, present in animal and plant cells, appears to inhibit the growth of cancer cells by changing the cells to make them become more normal. Raw vegetables, especially broccoli, cabbage and cauliflower and those high in dietary fibre, contain IP6 in abundance.

There is some evidence that **omega-3 fatty acids** may have specific benefits for cancer patients undergoing

chemotherapy, reducing the growth of tumours. Omega-3 fatty acids, which are essential to human health, are not produced by the body and must therefore be obtained from food. They can be found in fish such as bass, cod, halibut, herring, mackerel, salmon, sardines, shark and tuna. Omega-3 fatty acids can also be found in plants – they are then called alpha-linolenic acid (ALA). ALA can be found in flaxseed, kidney and soya beans.

Foods high in **protein** are important because protein helps build and repair tissue, retain muscle mass and also maintain a healthy immune system. Following surgery and during cancer treatment, additional protein is usually needed to heal tissue and help prevent infection. The best choices to meet protein needs are foods that are low in saturated fat. Good sources are eggs, fish, lean meat, legumes, non-fat and low-fat dairy products, nuts, poultry, pulses, seeds and soya products.

Research has confirmed that **honey** has healing properties. It can kill bacteria and is helpful in supporting the immune system. The sweet recipes in this book use honey rather than sugar where possible.

what to avoid

Try to eliminate processed, refined foods and stick to fresh, organic ingredients if possible. Read all labels carefully to make sure that food contains no chemical additives. Freshly cooked ham is one thing; supermarket ham in a packet with preservatives is another. Refined sugar and sweeteners such as aspartame, which is frequently found in yogurts, cereals and ready-made meals, have been linked to a range of diseases including cancer and are best avoided.

advice for specific cancer types

Always consult your specialist and oncology dietitian about what you should and shouldn't eat with your type of cancer.

Patients with **head and neck cancers**, including oesophageal and gastric cancers, invariably need extra nutritional support. A dry mouth is often seen and requires soft or very moist foods. Some patients prefer strong-flavoured foods. Tart foods can help increase the production of saliva. However, acidic or spicy foods are often not well tolerated. Ice-cold grapes and melon, eaten straight from the fridge in small quantities, make great snacks.

Patients with **upper gastro-intestinal cancer** run the risk of malnutrition due to chronic bowel discomfort resulting in diarrhoea and an irritable bowel. Dried beans, dried fruit, high-fibre cereals, milk and milk products, nuts, popcorn, seeds and sweetcorn are best avoided. Eat low-residue, low-fibre foods such as apple sauce, bananas, rice and toast. Avoid dehydration by drinking as much as you can, starting with sips and increasing the volume until you stop feeling comfortable. Dehydration salts may help.

Patients with **prostate and breast cancers**, both hormone-related cancers, may benefit from a milk- and dairy-free diet. Some people think that the hormones meant for the benefit of young calves, which are often present in dairy products, are the culprit. Certainly in China, where people eat a predominantly dairy-free diet, very few prostate and breast cancers are observed. Patients with these cancers may want to reduce their intake of milk products by using currently available alternatives, such as coconut, oat, rice and soya milk.

dietary supplements

Scientific evidence for the use of dietary supplements is currently inconclusive. Some cancer experts advise against taking supplements with antioxidant activity during treatment, claiming they could counteract the effectiveness of the chemotherapy. According to these scientists, antioxidants present in food should provide all the patient needs. However, other researchers believe that there may be benefits in taking supplementary antioxidants, to help protect normal cells from the damage the chemotherapy causes. When treatment has finished some practitioners recommend supplements. Always check with your oncologist before taking them.

what's the problem?

Once you have been diagnosed with cancer, chemotherapy may be offered as a treatment, but it will nearly always bring with it some less than pleasant side effects. One that will have a profound impact on your daily life is the marked change in your appreciation of food. Not only the cancer itself but also the side effects of treatment will affect your eating habits.

Different types of cancer have different effects on eating. Nausea, vomiting and diarrhoea are a particular problem; many people lose weight through malnourishment because they cannot keep their food down. As a result they get weaker and their recovery is adversely affected. If your specific cancer affects the mouth, throat or digestive system, it is likely to significantly reduce your appetite too.

The side effects of chemotherapy and radiotherapy are bound to have a major impact as well. The mouth can become dry as production of saliva diminishes. Mucous membranes can be badly affected, making swallowing difficult and sometimes painful. Blisters can make the mouth and throat dry and sore, affecting the way the mouth feels, and certain types of medication will cause constipation. In other words, you will be presented with a set of circumstances that makes the thought of eating unattractive and at times even repulsive.

all your senses are in disarray

On top of that, the tastes you are so familiar with – sweet, sour, bitter, salty – will seem to have changed. Instead of the sensations and experiences you're used to, completely new ones manifest themselves, and very often they are not agreeable. All of a sudden your favourite dishes, snacks and even fruit may taste awful. Normal tap water may acquire an acidic taste and spicy flavours may be transformed into something profoundly bitter. For some patients, orange juice, which is known to be very healthy, seems to burn its way down their throat into the stomach.

Other senses may be affected as well. The smell of food can be very disturbing and may cause nausea or vomiting. The sight of a plate heaped with food, or watching others enjoying big plates of food, can put you off completely.

It is not only the physical difficulties you are facing that make mealtimes a challenge; there is also a psychological dimension. After the diagnosis you may feel threatened, confused and afraid, rebellious or completely shocked and in denial. So eating easily becomes an issue: something that's difficult and painful to do and that adds more fear and confusion to an already deeply unpleasant situation.

making the best of a difficult situation

Meals have acquired a wider social function in our society. Breakfast, lunch and dinner are times to exchange feelings and the experiences of the day and are important for everyone involved. When one of those people is being treated for cancer, the menu requires careful consideration. Whoever is cooking needs to be aware of the kinds of food the patient can have and may feel like – this can vary from treatment to treatment and from day to day. In most cases, it's a matter of finding the right texture and temperature, together with determining the preference for savoury or sweet. In other words, it's a question of trial and error to discover what suits best.

Eating patterns will be unpredictable. Many patients feel embarrassed and worry about letting the cook down by eating just a mouthful. They may not even be able to eat at all, or may change their minds and prefer something else. Normal mealtimes no longer apply, and you'll eat what you can, when you can. The good news is that most side effects disappear shortly after finishing the treatment.

the aims of this book are:

1 To stimulate patients undergoing chemotherapy and radiotherapy to eat what they can when they can, in order to prevent weight loss and to keep up their strength as much as possible.

2 To ensure that the ingredients used in cooking for those undergoing chemotherapy and radiotherapy are beneficial to the patient.

3 To provide support, encouragement and inspiration to those cooking for someone undergoing cancer treatment.

4 To help the patient to enjoy their food and drink as much as possible within the limits of the treatment.

the method

This is a book with a mission. It aims to help patients and carers overcome – as best as possible – the various eating problems commonly associated with chemotherapy and radiotherapy: a painful mouth, a dry throat, a sensitive digestive system, difficulty in swallowing, loss of appetite and nausea. During treatment the intensity of these problems will vary with the effect of the chemicals and radiation on the body and on the mind.

The method devised involves structuring each chapter in such a way that it follows the preferences of most cancer patients when it comes to choosing what to eat. By adhering to this structure, patients and carers can easily pick the dishes that are best suited to patients' likes and needs, thus increasing the chance that they will actually want to eat the food prepared for them. They may even enjoy it!

texture

During and after treatment a patient's sense of taste and smell will be unreliable. To increase the likelihood of patients eating food – any food – carers need to focus on the food's texture and temperature, rather than on ingredients. Therefore the chapters in this book are divided into six textures, each offering healthy, nourishing dishes.

LIGHT
The dishes in this chapter are characterised by their fluffy, soft texture. When eating a Light recipe, it isn't necessary to chew, so even patients with a sore mouth or throat can eat them.

SMOOTH
With their creamy texture, the dishes in this chapter slip down easily when chewing and even swallowing are difficult because of an extremely dry, sore mouth and throat.

SOFT WITH A BITE
These dishes can be eaten when chewing isn't the biggest problem and the mouth and throat are not too sore. Even for patients with a fairly dry mouth, most of them are easy to cope with.

LIQUID
For patients with a badly affected mouth and throat who find chewing and swallowing painful, liquid 'foods' like the dishes in this chapter are a suitable option.

CRISPY
Crispness has a great influence on the appetite – it might just persuade people who have no craving for food whatsoever to take a bite. Crispy food will only work when mouth and throat are not sore, painful or dry and when chewing and swallowing are not a problem.

FIRM
These dishes bring back a semblance of everyday food, but the portions remain small so they don't overwhelm patients by their sheer bulk. They are suitable when the throat and mouth are not too affected and chewing and swallowing are possible.

temperature

After texture, patients are most likely to prefer a certain temperature – cold or warm. Every chapter therefore moves from a selection of cold dishes (both savoury and sweet) to warm dishes (also savoury and sweet).

The sweet dishes aren't desserts as such but 'meals' in their own right, just like the savoury dishes. Remember, it's what patients can eat and want to eat that's important; if that means eating sweet dishes only, so be it. This explains why you'll find sweet dishes scattered throughout the chapters rather than at the back of each chapter, as you might expect in a traditional cookery book.

flavour

Finally, every chapter offers a selection of mild dishes and dishes that are stronger-tasting, to cater for a wide range of patients, from those who have become very sensitive to flavours to those whose sense of taste has diminished.

The arrangement of the recipes in each chapter is therefore:

- cool and savoury with a mild flavour
- cool and savoury with a strong flavour
- cool and sweet
- warm and savoury with a mild flavour
- warm and savoury with a strong flavour
- warm and sweet

portion size

Many cancer patients undergoing chemotherapy and radiotherapy feel intimidated when large amounts of food are placed in front of them. Because their sensory system is completely off balance, a loaded plate represents an avalanche of smells, flavours and colours that is often threatening and can cause a complete mental block against food.

It is much easier for patients to eat small meals at various times of the day. You will find that the recipes in this book all make two or three small portions. By eating together, patients and carers will have the opportunity to share an important part of their day and this may bring back some of the enjoyment of food. Although freshly prepared food offers the best nutritional value, it is possible to keep most dishes for a day or two in the fridge or to freeze them.

hygiene

People undergoing invasive treatments have a compromised immune system. Anyone cooking for them needs to be particularly aware of food hygiene, making sure all fruit and vegetables, tools, cutting boards, cutlery and plates are cleaned thoroughly. Tea towels and dishcloths must be changed after every use and washed on a high temperature.

about the recipes

The recipes in this book have been developed for cancer patients of (almost) all ages: youngsters (but not babies or small children), adolescents, adults and the elderly.

In most cases, if you want to stimulate patients to eat, the trick is to find food with the right texture and temperature, establishing a preference for savoury or sweet.

Recipes have been kept as simple and inspiring as possible, focusing on fresh, healthy ingredients. Other members of the family might easily be tempted to join in. To allow for this, each recipe also gives the ingredients needed to feed a family of four, including the patient.

The ultimate aim is clear: to ensure the intake of as much essential food as possible under the circumstances. Always remember, anything is better than nothing!

will it work?

The method described in this book will not work for everybody – each patient is different, circumstances vary and not everybody reacts to cancer therapies in a predictable way. That said, it will help in identifying dishes that are as suitable as possible for individual patients. However, in situations when no food can be eaten at all, malnourishment becomes a serious risk. In that case, supplements and even stomach tube feeding will probably be considered.

the good foods list

Highly recommended

Apricots
Artichokes
Asparagus
Avocados
Bananas
Beans
Beetroot
Berries
Blackcurrants
Brazil nuts
Brewer's yeast
Broccoli
Cabbage
Carrots
Cauliflower
Cereals
Cherries
Citrus fruits, including zest (except grapefruit)
Cod
Cranberries
Eggs
Fish
Flaxseed oil
Game
Garlic

Ginger
Grains
Grapes
Halibut
Herring
Kiwi fruit
Lean meat
Leeks
Linseed oil
Mackerel
Melons
Nuts
Oily fish
Olive oil
Onions
Organic food
Parsley
Peaches
Peppers
Pomegranate juice
Poultry
Pulses
Pumpkin
Rhubarb
Rosehip
Salmon

Sardines
Sea bass
Seeds
Sesame seeds
Shark
Shellfish
Shiitake mushrooms
Soya products
Spinach
Spirulina (available in health shops)
Squash
Sunflower seeds
Sweet potatoes
Tea: green and white, herbal teas, rooibos
Tomatoes
Tuna
Turmeric
Vegetables
Wheat germ

Use occasionally

Butter	Honey
Coffee	Pâté
Dairy products: non- and low-fat are best (none for patients with breast and prostate cancers)	Red meat
	Red wine
	Salt and sea salt
	Saturated fats
	Smoked foods
Deep-fried foods (fried only in extra virgin olive oil at the right temperature)	Sugar
	Whisky (only good malt whisky)

Avoid

Alcohol (most types, except red wine and good malt whisky)	Fizzy drinks
	Grapefruit
Barbecued or burnt foods	Margarine: hydrogenated or partly hydrogenated
Biscuits (when not home-made with good ingredients)	Processed foods, e.g. cheese, sausages, hot dogs, ham
Cakes (when not home-made with good ingredients)	Sweeteners
	White bread
Doughnuts	White refined flour
Fast foods	

hints and tips

eating and drinking

◈ Appetite is likely to fluctuate wildly, so embrace any occasion when patients want to eat, even if it's the middle of the night!

◈ Some people will eat better at certain times of day, so try to find out the optimum times for them.

◈ The sight of big portions can be nauseating, so small portions are recommended – and not just for patients, but for those eating with them too. If a patient's appetite increases, you can always enlarge the portions (simply multiply the quantities by two or three), or serve seconds.

◈ To make food taste better, patients can try rinsing their mouth with water before eating, or brushing their tongue lightly with a wet toothbrush.

◈ Try to eat slowly and chew well to help digestion.

◈ It is important to keep the body's fluid level up, so keep sipping water or green tea whatever your symptoms. Try to avoid drinking at the same time as eating.

◈ If you suffer from nausea or vomiting, avoid cooking smells. Wear comfortable, loose-fitting clothes and keep your head upright after eating.

◈ Conventional knives and forks may leave an unpleasant, metallic taste in the mouth. Using plastic knives and forks is a good solution.

◈ Anaesthetic sprays are now available for patients to use in the mouth and throat to enable them to eat more easily.

◈ Keep healthy snacks close at hand for nibbling when required. Snack ideas are scattered throughout the book.

in hospital

◈ Eat a very light meal before your treatment, or take a snack with you to eat while travelling to hospital if the journey is long.

◈ It is recommended that you drink water both before and during chemotherapy. Keep this up for a couple of days after treatment to flush the chemicals through. Aim to drink between eight and ten glasses per day. Green tea is also excellent.

◈ Avoid eating directly after treatment for a few hours.

choosing the right dish

◈ Finding which foods suit patients best will be a case of trial and error. Using the method recommended in this book, focusing on texture first, then temperature and flavours, can be the key to success.

◈ Experience with cancer patients has shown that there's often an initial preference for a sweetish taste, even in savoury dishes. Many recipes in this book therefore have a sweet element to them.

◈ Smell and presentation are two other important factors that influence the appreciation of food. Try to find out what appeals and what repels.

◈ Whenever you sense an appreciation for certain tastes or textures, try to expand on it.

◈ The type of food that achieves the best results during treatment is often very difficult to pinpoint and may change over time. Keep on trying and always be flexible.

❧ Whenever possible, choose ingredients that are considered beneficial to cancer patients in general and to the type of cancer concerned in particular. The Good Foods List (see page 20) can help.

❧ Try to avoid the foods that are advised against (see pages 12 and 21) if you can. However, sometimes you will have to compromise – it's better for the patient to be eating something rather than nothing. If necessary, sparingly use non-recommended ingredients like fructose or even sugar – they could prove to be the irresistible ingredient that makes a recipe work.

❧ Tart foods are often pleasing to those with dry mouths – they stimulate the production of saliva.

❧ If eating or drinking dairy products results in heightened mucus production, you'd better choose savoury dishes using dairy products as the salt in savoury foods has a clearing effect on the mucus.

❧ If you suffer from nausea and vomiting, bland foods and mild flavours are often wise choices. Eating dry foods first thing in the morning may help. Ginger can also be effective in controlling nausea – try ginger ale, ginger tea or ginger biscuits.

❧ When the sense of taste has all but disappeared, try seasoning dishes more strongly than usual, or choose a strong-flavoured recipe from this book, in order to provide some sort of taste distinction.

❧ Gas, bloating and cramping can be helped by eating little and often, and avoiding fizzy drinks and drinking through a straw.

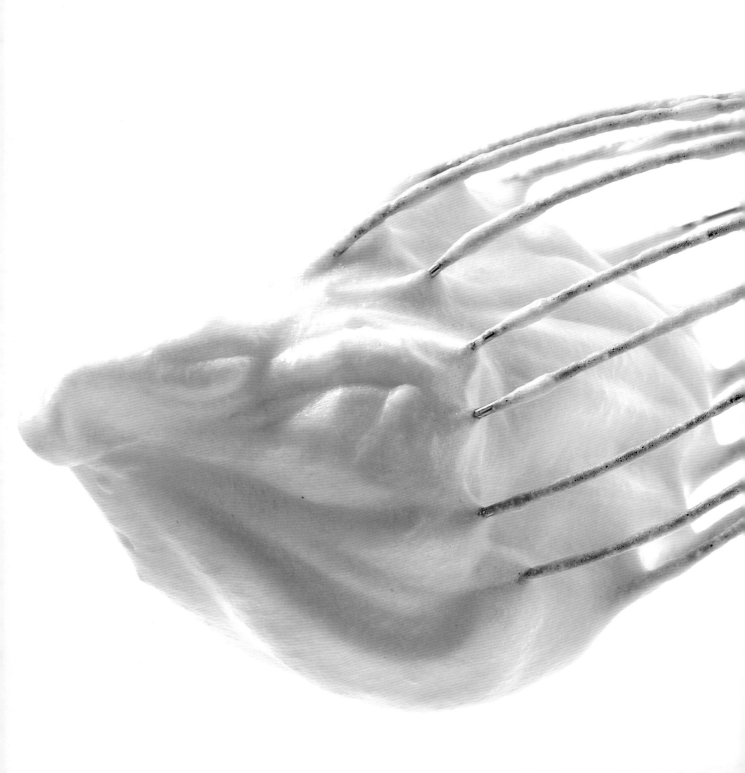

chapter one

light

carrot cream

This can also be made with pumpkin, beetroot, cauliflower or broccoli instead of carrots. Try adding a little chopped fresh ginger and replacing the honey with ginger syrup. For more flavour, turmeric or curry powder may be added to taste.

5 small carrots
1 small onion
1 garlic clove
1 orange
1/2 slice wholemeal bread
3 sprigs of fresh parsley
splash of olive oil

honey
pinch of salt
pinch of pepper
4 tablespoons live or soya
    yogurt

2 small portions

Peel and chop the carrots. Peel and chop the onion and garlic. Wash the orange, grate the zest and squeeze out the juice. Remove the bread crusts and cut the bread into small cubes. Chop the parsley finely.

Heat splash of olive oil in a saucepan. Add the carrots, onion, garlic and orange zest and fry for 3 minutes over a medium heat. Add the bread cubes, orange juice and just enough water to cover the carrots. Cook until the carrots are very soft, 10–15 minutes.

Whizz in a blender or food-processor to a smooth purée. Add 1/2–1 teaspoon honey, salt and pepper to taste and set aside to cool.

Whisk the yogurt and carrot purée together. Add three-quarters of the parsley, adjust the seasoning to taste and whisk for a further few minutes.

Spoon into small bowls or glasses and sprinkle with the rest of the parsley.

FOR A FAMILY OF FOUR:
MULTIPLY THE INGREDIENTS BY SIX AND SERVE AS A STARTER OR AS
A SIDE DISH WITH FISH OR POULTRY.

beetroot and goat's cheese whip

Good balsamic vinegar is slightly sweet and soft at the same time. It goes very well with beetroot but can be replaced by any other vinegar. If you choose to do this, add some extra honey to get a nice sweet and sour balance.

sprig of fresh parsley
1 small cooked beetroot
8 tablespoons (about 75g) fresh
    goat's cheese or soya yogurt
$^1/_2$–1 teaspoon honey
$^1/_2$ tablespoon balsamic vinegar
salt and pepper

2 small portions

Chop the parsley very finely.

Whizz the beetroot in a blender or food-processor. Ensure the purée is as fine as possible. Add all the other ingredients except the parsley and whizz for a few more minutes until the mixture is light and fluffy. Adjust the seasoning to taste.

Spoon into small bowls or glasses and sprinkle with the parsley.

Tip: This recipe can also be made with cooked carrots, pumpkin, courgette or aubergine.

FOR A FAMILY OF FOUR:
MULTIPLY THE INGREDIENTS BY FOUR AND SERVE AS A STARTER.

fluffy tomato cream

This cream is finished off by sprinkling some chopped chives on top. The chives can also be mixed into the cream, and celery leaf or dill can be used instead of chives.

2 stems of fresh chives
8 tablespoons whipping or soya cream
2 tablespoons live or soya yogurt
150ml passata
pinch of salt
pinch of pepper
pinch of curry powder

2 small portions

Chop the chives very finely.

Whip the cream with the yogurt, passata, a pinch of salt, a pinch of pepper and a pinch of curry powder until creamy and fluffy.

Divide the cream between two small glasses and sprinkle the chives on top.

Tip: Curry powder is optional. It contains turmeric, so you can use just turmeric instead of curry powder if you prefer.

FOR A FAMILY OF FOUR:
MULTIPLY THE INGREDIENTS BY FOUR AND SERVE AS A STARTER.

snacks

Recommended ready-to-eat light and soft snacks are terrines and fish mousses, such as salmon and sweet mousses. When buying ready-made snacks, try and go for ones without preservatives and preferably without hydrogenated fats. Try to buy organic products if at all possible.

smoked chicken and almond mousse

This dish can be prepared in advance, but it is better to whip and add the cream just before serving.

about 50g smoked chicken
2 tablespoons ground almonds
$^1/_2$ tablespoon mayonnaise
$^1/_2$ tablespoon tomato ketchup
salt and pepper
5 tablespoons whipping or soya cream

2 small portions

Whizz the chicken and ground almonds together in a blender or food-processor. Make sure that the mixture is as fine as possible. Transfer to a bowl and stir in the mayonnaise and ketchup. Add salt and pepper to taste.

Whip the cream until fluffy. Fold it into the chicken mixture.

Divide the mousse between two small dishes.

Tip: Soya cream will not get as stiff as whipping cream. It may be replaced by live or soya yogurt. However, then the mousse will not be as fluffy.

FOR A FAMILY OF FOUR:
MULTIPLY THE INGREDIENTS BY FOUR AND SERVE AS A STARTER.

whipped tuna with orange

For the right texture, the tuna and orange mixture should be whizzed until very fine. If necessary, pass it through a sieve before serving. Instead of tuna, cooked or tinned salmon or cooked prawns can be used.

4 tablespoons cooked or tinned tuna
4 tablespoons fresh orange juice
1/2 tablespoon mayonnaise
1 tablespoon live or soya yogurt
5 tablespoons whipping or soya cream
pinch of salt
pinch of pepper

2 small portions

Whizz the tuna and orange juice together in a blender or food-processor. Make sure the mixture is as fine as possible. Add the other ingredients and whizz for a few more minutes until the mixture is light and fluffy.

Divide the mousse between glasses.

Tip: Since orange zest is considered to be healthy and is also very tasty, you may want to add some to this dish.

FOR A FAMILY OF FOUR:
MULTIPLY THE INGREDIENTS BY FOUR AND SERVE AS A STARTER.

light blueberry yogurt cream

Other berries or soft fruit may be used instead of fresh blueberries. This recipe also works well with frozen fruit, though you must defrost the fruit first. Instead of honey, a 100% fruit jam (with no added sugar) may be used to sweeten the cream.

100g blueberries
150ml live or soya yogurt
$1/2$–1 tablespoon honey
5 tablespoons whipping or soya cream

2 small portions

Wash the blueberries thoroughly and pat them dry with some kitchen paper.

Whizz the blueberries in a blender or food-processor. Ensure the purée is as fine as possible. Add the yogurt and honey to taste and whizz for a minute longer.

Whip the cream in a big bowl. (Soya cream will not get as stiff as whipping cream.) Add the blueberry mixture and fold it into the cream.

Divide the cream between two glasses.

FOR A FAMILY OF FOUR:
MULTIPLY THE RECIPE BY FOUR AND SERVE AS A DESSERT.

cream of fig and banana

To prevent the banana from discolouring, you can sprinkle it with some lemon juice. If you do, add a tiny bit of extra honey to make sure the cream is sweet enough.

2 dried figs
1/2 banana
150ml live or soya yogurt
1/2–1 teaspoon honey
5 tablespoons whipping or soya cream

2 small portions

Cut off the hard 'stem' of the figs and peel the banana.

Whizz the figs and banana in a blender or food-processor to a very fine purée. Add the yogurt and the honey and whizz for a minute longer.

Whip the cream in a big bowl. (Soya cream will not get as stiff as whipping cream.) Add the banana mixture and fold it into the cream.

Divide the cream between two small bowls or glasses.

Tip: The dried figs may be replaced by dates or prunes.

FOR A FAMILY OF FOUR:
MULTIPLY THE INGREDIENTS BY FOUR AND SERVE AS A DESSERT.

apple and cinnamon whip

It is easiest to use apple sauce from a jar for this recipe. If you want to make fresh apple sauce, sweeten it with honey rather than sugar.

8 tablespoons apple sauce
3 scoops soft vanilla ice cream
1/2 teaspoon ground cinnamon

2 small portions

Whizz all the ingredients together in a blender or food-processor until smooth and fluffy.

Divide between two glasses.

Tip: Apple sauce may be replaced by apricot compote.

FOR A FAMILY OF FOUR:
MULTIPLY THE INGREDIENTS BY THREE AND SERVE AS A DESSERT.

raspberry mousse

This mousse is quite soft and can be drunk through a thick straw. If raspberry seeds are going to be a problem, you may want to pass the purée through a sieve before folding it in with the whipped cream.

100g raspberries
100ml ready-made custard
1 teaspoon honey
5 tablespoons whipping or soya cream

2 small portions

Wash the raspberries carefully and pat them dry with some kitchen paper.

Whizz the raspberries in a blender or food-processor. Ensure the purée is as fine as possible. Add the custard and honey and whizz for a minute longer.

Whip the cream in a big bowl. Add the raspberry mixture and fold it into the cream.

Divide the mousse between two small bowls or glasses.

Tip: Soya cream will not get as stiff as whipping cream. It may be replaced by live or soya yogurt, in which case the mousse will not be quite as fluffy.

FOR A FAMILY OF FOUR:
MULTIPLY THE INGREDIENTS BY FOUR AND SERVE AS A DESSERT.

turkey, walnut and spinach mousse

In this recipe the mousse is prepared with fresh spinach. You could use about 30g frozen spinach instead – add it to the turkey and heat until it is defrosted and hot.

about 50g turkey fillet
splash of olive oil
pinch of salt
pinch of pepper
about 50g fresh spinach
1 egg
2 tablespoons shelled walnuts
1 slice wholemeal bread
2 tablespoons crème fraîche
  or soya cream

2–3 small portions

Preheat the oven to 180°C/350°F/gas mark 4.

Cut the turkey into small pieces.

Heat a splash of olive oil in a big frying pan. Add the turkey, a pinch of salt and pepper and fry for 5 minutes. Add the spinach and stir-fry for 3 minutes.

Separate the egg.

Whizz the walnuts in a blender or food-processor until very fine. Add the bread and whizz to make breadcrumbs. Add the turkey mixture, crème fraîche and egg yolk. Whizz to a smooth cream.

Beat the egg white with a pinch of salt until stiff. Fold into the turkey mixture. Divide the mixture between two or three small greased oven dishes, such as ramekins, and bake in the oven for 15 minutes until just set.

Serve hot.

Tip: The crème fraîche can be replaced by fresh goat's cheese.

FOR A FAMILY OF FOUR:
MULTIPLY THE RECIPE BY THREE AND SERVE AS A STARTER.

the benefits of olive oil

In cold dishes, use linseed oil or olive oil, since they are the best for your digestive system. In hot dishes, use only extra virgin olive oil since it is considered to be the best for your health.

aubergine herby mousse

This mousse can be enjoyed both hot and cold, and it can also be used as a dip for vegetables and bread.

1 spring onion
1/4 aubergine
splash of olive oil
pinch of salt
pinch of pepper
1 egg
1/2 slice wholemeal bread

sprig of fresh parsley
stem of fresh chives
sprig of fresh dill
1 plum tomato (tinned)

2 small portions

Wash and chop the spring onion. Wash the aubergine and cut into pieces.

Heat a splash of olive oil in a big frying pan, add the spring onion and fry for 2 minutes on a medium heat. Add the aubergine and fry for 5 minutes on a low heat. Add a pinch each of salt and pepper.

Separate the egg.

Whizz the bread and herbs in a blender or food-processor to make herby breadcrumbs. Add the tomato, aubergine mixture and egg yolk and whizz to a very fine, smooth cream.

Put the mixture in a double boiler (or simply a bowl) over simmering water and cook, stirring constantly, for about 5 minutes. Season to taste.

Beat the egg white until stiff. Fold into the aubergine mixture and cook for a few more minutes.

Divide between two small dishes and serve immediately.

Tip: As an additional fresh touch, you can serve this mousse with some live or soya yogurt on the side.

FOR A FAMILY OF FOUR:
MULTIPLY THE INGREDIENTS BY THREE, BUT USE A WHOLE SMALL AUBERGINE.
SERVE AS A STARTER OR SIDE DISH.

steamed chicken, apricot and curry mousse

Try smoked chicken or cooked ham instead of fresh chicken. Turmeric can also be added if you like.

1 small onion
about 50g chicken fillet
2 ready-to-eat dried apricots
splash of olive oil
pinch of salt
pinch of pepper
pinch of curry powder
1 egg
1/2 slice wholemeal bread

2 small portions

Peel and chop the onion. Cut the chicken and apricots into small pieces.

Heat a splash of olive oil in a frying pan, add the onion and fry for 3 minutes on a medium heat. Add the chicken, a pinch of salt, a pinch of pepper and a pinch of curry powder. Fry for a further 5 minutes.

Separate the egg.

Whizz the bread in a blender or food-processor to make breadcrumbs. Add the chicken mixture, apricots and egg yolk and whizz to a smooth cream.

Beat the egg white with a pinch of salt until stiff. Fold into the chicken mixture.

Divide the mixture between two small greased oven dishes such as ramekins. Cover the dishes with foil, place on a steaming rack in a pan over boiling water and cover the pan. Steam for about 10 minutes until just set.

Place the dishes on small plates and serve warm.

Tip: It is strongly recommended that you use wholemeal bread, even though it makes the mousse a bit less light. You can use white bread, but it is not so healthy.

FOR A FAMILY OF FOUR:
MULTIPLY THE RECIPE BY FOUR AND SERVE AS A STARTER.

creamy fish soufflé

Unlike white fish, mackerel contains essential fatty acids. For a change you could also try other fatty fish, such as trout, salmon or tuna.

2 eggs
1/2 slice wholemeal bread
3 sprigs of fresh parsley
75g steamed or smoked
    mackerel fillet
1 grilled red pepper from a jar
salt and pepper

2 small portions

Preheat the oven to 220°C/425°F/gas mark 7.

Separate the eggs.

Whizz the bread and parsley in a blender or food-processor to make herby breadcrumbs. Add the mackerel, red pepper and egg yolks and whizz to a smooth cream. Season to taste.

Beat the egg whites with a pinch of salt until stiff. Fold into the fish mixture.

Divide the mixture between two small greased oven dishes, such as ramekins, and bake in the oven for 15 minutes until just set.

Serve immediately.

Tip: You could use a fresh red pepper and grill it yourself, but make sure it doesn't blacken when it's in the oven. Put it in a plastic bag when soft. Close the bag and let the pepper cool. Skin, cut into pieces and mix them with a dash of vinegar and a few drops of honey.

FOR A FAMILY OF FOUR:
MULTIPLY THE INGREDIENTS BY THREE AND SERVE AS A STARTER.

mushroom mousse

This is like a soufflé and is baked in the oven. It can also be steamed or prepared in a double boiler.

150g mushrooms
1 small onion
1 garlic clove
splash of olive oil

1 egg
1 thin slice wholemeal bread
salt and pepper

2 small portions

Preheat the oven to 180°C/350°F/gas mark 4.

Wipe the mushrooms clean and chop them. Peel and chop the onion and garlic.

Heat a splash of olive oil in a big frying pan, add the onion and fry for 3 minutes on a medium heat. Add the garlic and mushrooms and fry for a further 5 minutes.

Separate the egg.

Whizz the bread in a blender or food-processor to make breadcrumbs. Add the mushroom mixture and the egg yolk and whizz to a smooth cream. Add salt and pepper to taste.

Beat the egg white with a pinch of salt until stiff. Fold into the mushroom mixture.

Divide the mixture between two small greased oven dishes, such as egg cups or ramekins, and bake in the oven for 15 minutes until just set.

Serve hot.

Tip: This recipe can be made with any type of edible mushroom or mushroom mixture. Shiitake mushrooms are particularly good.

FOR A FAMILY OF FOUR:
DOUBLE THE INGREDIENTS AND SERVE AS A STARTER.

floating islands with peach melba swirl

These 'floating islands' are made in the oven because it is so easy. However, you can also prepare them in almost-boiling water. Just add two or three scoops of the mixture at a time and 'cook' them for a few minutes.

1 egg white
25g sugar
pinch of salt
1 ripe peach
1/2–1 teaspoon honey
50g fresh or frozen raspberries

2–3 small portions

Preheat the oven to 100°C/210°F/gas mark 1/4.

Beat the egg white with the sugar and a pinch of salt until very stiff. Cover a baking tray with baking paper, and place 6–9 spoonfuls of egg white on to the tray. Ensure there is plenty of space between them. Bake in the oven for about 1 1/2 hours.

Skin the peach, then whizz in a blender or food-processor to a fine purée. If raspberry seeds are going to be a problem, you may want to pass the purée through a sieve. Sweeten with a little honey and pour into a small saucepan.

Wash the raspberries and dry them with kitchen paper. Place the raspberries in the blender or food-processor (it doesn't have to be cleaned after the peaches). Whizz to a fine purée and sweeten with a little honey. Pour into another saucepan.

Heat both purées. Pour the peach purée into two or three small wide dishes. Add the raspberry purée and pass a knife through it to get the swirl effect. Place the egg-white 'islands' on top.

Tip: To ensure that egg whites will properly stiffen when beaten, make certain the kitchen tools used are grease-free by wiping them with kitchen paper sprinkled with vinegar.

FOR A FAMILY OF FOUR:
DOUBLE THE INGREDIENTS AND SERVE AS A DESSERT.

substituting ingredients

It isn't always necessary to follow recipes to the letter. If you don't have an ingredient to hand, most of the time you can substitute it with something similar. For instance, in this recipe, mango can be used instead of peach.

baked vanilla mousse

This recipe can also be made with chocolate but it will not be as light. To make chocolate mousse, do not use lemon juice. Melt 50g chocolate with the cream and half a tablespoon of honey (instead of vanilla sugar) over a low heat.

1 egg
2 tablespoons custard powder
5 tablespoons whipping or
  soya cream

2 tablespoons vanilla sugar
splash of lemon juice
pinch of salt

2 small portions

Preheat the oven to 160°C/325°F/gas mark 3.

Separate the egg.

Mix the custard powder with 1 tablespoon of water.

Whisk the egg yolk with the custard powder, cream, vanilla sugar and lemon juice until the sugar has dissolved.

Beat the egg white with a pinch of salt until stiff. Fold into the vanilla mixture.

Pour into two small greased oven dishes and bake in the oven for 20 minutes until just set.

Serve warm or cold.

Tip: Instead of vanilla sugar, you can use honey as a sweetener. In this case, add a drop of vanilla essence to the mixture.

FOR A FAMILY OF FOUR:
MULTIPLY THE INGREDIENTS BY THREE AND SERVE AS A DESSERT.

warm cranberry and honey mousse

Sugarless cranberry juice is good for patients having abdominal radiotherapy, which affects the bladder and can cause radiation cystitis. However, cranberries can exaggerate the negative effects of warfarin (a blood thinner or anticoagulant) so don't use cranberry juice if you are taking warfarin.

100ml cranberry juice
3 tablespoons honey
1 tablespoon cornflour
2 egg whites
5 tablespoons whipping or soya cream

2 small portions

Pour the cranberry juice into a pan. Add the honey, bring to a boil and reduce by half.

Mix the cornflour with 1 tablespoon of water in a pan. Whisk in the egg whites, the cream and the cranberry mixture.

Put the mixture in a double boiler or a bowl over simmering water and whisk until the mixture is thick and creamy, for about 5 minutes.

Divide between two glasses and serve immediately.

Tip: Cranberry juice can be bought ready-made or you can make it yourself by boiling cranberries with an equal amount of water. Strain and sweeten to taste if necessary. The cranberry juice can be replaced by other juices such as pomegranate, redcurrant, blueberry or orange.

FOR A FAMILY OF FOUR:
MULTIPLY THE INGREDIENTS BY THREE
AND SERVE AS A DESSERT.

hot lemon mousse

In this recipe, the mousse is prepared in a double boiler and must be whisked for about 10 minutes. Make sure the pan with the lemon mixture is in a stable position so no water from the lower pan can get into it. The whisking can be done either by hand or with an electric mixer.

1 small lemon
1 tablespoon honey
1/2 tablespoon custard powder
2 eggs
5 tablespoons whipping or
   soya cream

2–3 small portions

Squeeze the lemon to obtain the juice and pour into a pan. Add the honey, bring to a boil and reduce to half. Place the pan over another pan containing simmering water.

Mix the custard powder with 1 tablespoon of water. Stir into the lemon mixture. Beat in the eggs and keep on beating until the mixture is thick and creamy, for 5–10 minutes.

Whip the cream and at the last moment fold it into the lemon mousse.

Divide between two or three dishes and serve immediately.

Tip: Orange or lime juice can be used instead of lemon juice.

FOR A FAMILY OF FOUR:
MULTIPLY THE RECIPE BY THREE AND SERVE AS A DESSERT.

special foods for different cancers

You should always consult your specialist and the oncology dietician about what you should and shouldn't eat depending on your type of cancer.

chapter two
smooth

creamed asparagus and prawns

Green asparagus may be used instead of white asparagus. The fresh dill can be left out or replaced with parsley, fennel or chervil.

sprig of fresh dill
5 thin and small white asparagus,
    tinned or freshly cooked
1/2 slice wholemeal bread
about 100g cooked prawns
1 tablespoon mayonnaise
a few drops of fresh lemon juice
pinch of salt
pinch of pepper

2 small portions

Chop the dill very finely.

Peel the asparagus thinly, if using fresh, and snap off the woody part of the stems by bending the stalks until they break naturally. Cook the fresh asparagus in salted water for 10–15 minutes, until soft, and then set aside to cool. Reserve 2 tablespoons of the cooking water.

Whizz the bread in a blender or food-processor to crumbs. Add the prawns, asparagus and 2 tablespoons of the cooking liquid if using fresh asparagus or 2 tablespoons of the liquid from the asparagus tin if using tinned. Whizz to a smooth cream. Mix in the mayonnaise, lemon juice, dill, a pinch of salt and a pinch of pepper.

Fill two small glasses or bowls with the cream.

FOR A FAMILY OF FOUR:
MULTIPLY THE INGREDIENTS BY FOUR AND SERVE AS A STARTER.

snacks

No matter which snacks you decide to serve, buy untreated products without preservatives where you can. Check the label for sugar content. Some of the best ready-to-eat smooth snacks include apple sauce, custard, fruit yogurt, rhubarb compote, ripe kaki fruit (also called persimmon or Sharon fruit), ripe plums and ripe melon.

avocado purée
with orange

It is always best to buy avocados when they are really ripe; experience shows that they don't ripen easily later and using them when they are still hard always leads to disappointment.

1 small ripe avocado
4 tablespoons orange juice
2 tablespoons sour or soya
    cream
pinch of salt
pinch of pepper

2–3 small portions

Halve the avocado, remove the stone and scoop out the pulp.

Whizz the avocado with the orange juice in a blender or food-processor to a smooth cream. Fold in the sour cream or live soya yogurt or mayonnaise. Add a pinch of salt and a pinch of pepper.

Fill two or three small glasses or dishes with the purée.

FOR A FAMILY OF FOUR:
DOUBLE THE INGREDIENTS AND SERVE AS A STARTER.

minced ratatouille

This recipe forms the basis for all sorts of vegetable dishes but it should always contain tomato. To accompany the tomato, choose vegetables with a firm texture such as carrot, broccoli or celeriac. You can also add chopped herbs.

1 small tomato
1/8 red pepper
1/4 courgette
1 small onion
1 garlic clove
1 small, sweet, pickled gherkin
2 tablespoons olive oil
salt and pepper
1/2 slice wholemeal bread
2 tablespoons sour cream
   (optional)

2 small portions

Wash the tomato, red pepper and courgette. Deseed the red pepper. Peel the onion and the garlic. Chop the vegetables, onion, garlic and gherkin into small pieces.

Heat the oil in a frying pan and fry the vegetables, onion, garlic and gherkin for 3 minutes on a medium heat, stirring constantly. Add salt and pepper to taste. Add 200ml water, turn down the heat and let the ratatouille simmer for 10 minutes.

Whizz the bread in a blender or food-processor into crumbs. Add the ratatouille and whizz to a smooth cream. Let it cool. Adjust the seasoning.

Divide the ratatouille between two small glasses or dishes. Serve cold with, if you wish, a spoonful of sour cream.

FOR A FAMILY OF FOUR:
MULTIPLY THE INGREDIENTS BY FOUR AND SERVE AS A STARTER.

shiitake mushroom cream

This cream can be enjoyed as it is, but it is also very nice with soft bread, on toast or in a small crêpe. By simply adding some stock, you can easily turn it into a soup.

75g mushrooms (button and
    some shiitake)
1/2 small onion
1/2 garlic clove
splash of olive oil
2 sprigs of fresh parsley

1/2 slice wholemeal bread
2 tablespoons crème fraîche
    or soya cream
salt and pepper

2 small portions

Wipe the mushrooms and chop them. Peel and chop the onion and garlic.

Heat a splash of olive oil in a big frying pan. Add the onion and mushrooms and fry for 5 minutes on a medium heat. Add the garlic and fry for a further 3 minutes.

Chop the parsley finely.

Whizz the bread in a blender or food-processor into crumbs. Add the mushrooms and parsley. Whizz to a smooth cream. Let it cool.

Add the crème fraîche to the mushroom cream and season to taste.

Fill two small dishes with the cream.

Tip: Instead of salt, a splash of soy sauce can be used to flavour this dish.

FOR A FAMILY OF FOUR:
MULTIPLY THE INGREDIENTS BY THREE AND SERVE AS A STARTER.

minted tuna and peas

Should an even smoother cream be required, making it easier to swallow, pass this cream through a fine sieve before adding mayonnaise.

100g fresh or frozen peas
sprig of fresh mint
6 tablespoons freshly cooked or
    tinned tuna

3 very small cocktail onions
1¹/₂ tablespoons mayonnaise

2 small portions

Cook the peas in boiling water for about 10 minutes until soft. Rinse with cold water and leave to cool.

Chop the mint leaves very finely.

Whizz the peas, tuna, cocktail onions and mint in a blender or food-processor to a smooth cream. Mix in the mayonnaise and a splash of the pickle liquid from the jar of onions.

Fill two small glasses or dishes with the cream.

Tip: As an alternative to tuna, you could use freshly cooked salmon or cooked prawns in this recipe.

FOR A FAMILY OF FOUR:
MULTIPLY THE INGREDIENTS BY THREE AND SERVE AS A STARTER.

panna cotta with honey and strawberries

This smooth and creamy pudding can be prepared up to two days in advance. However, its texture will stiffen slightly as time passes. The gelatine mixture should be cool but still fluid when adding it to the yogurt mixture. If it has already started to set, simply put it back on the heat so it will melt again.

3g gelatine powder or 2 sheets of gelatine
125ml whipping or soya cream
2 tablespoons honey
150ml live or soya yogurt
6 strawberries

2–3 small portions

Prepare or soak the gelatine according to the instructions on the packet.

Bring half of the cream and all of the honey to the boil in a small saucepan. Stir and take the pan off the heat. Stir in the gelatine and let it dissolve. Leave to cool, stirring every few minutes, until cool but not set.

Whip the remaining cream in the meantime until almost thick and spoon in the yogurt quickly. Stir into the gelatine mixture. Mix well but do it quickly. Pour into two or three small bowls or glasses. Leave in the fridge to set for at least 2 hours.

Clean and halve the strawberries, then sit them on the panna cottas.

Tip: Strawberries can be replaced with any other soft fruit you prefer, fresh or frozen.

FOR A FAMILY OF FOUR:
DOUBLE THIS RECIPE AND SERVE AS A DESSERT.

stop counting calories

During treatment it does not make much sense to be counting calories. Because eating is already difficult enough, it is better to concentrate on using as wide a variety of healthy ingredients as possible.

soft apple and cinnamon compote

This compote can be made with apples or with a mixture of apples and blackberries, blueberries or cranberries.

2 cooking apples
splash of lemon juice
1/2 tablespoon honey, or according to taste
pinch of cinnamon

2–3 small portions

Peel the apples, then halve, core and chop them.

Put the apples in a small saucepan with the lemon juice, honey, 3 tablespoons of water and the cinnamon. Cook over medium heat for 5–8 minutes, until the compote is very soft, stirring now and then. Leave to cool.

Fill two small glasses or dishes with the compote and sprinkle with a little more cinnamon.

FOR A FAMILY OF FOUR:
MULTIPLY THE INGREDIENTS BY THREE AND SERVE AS A DESSERT.

banana and lemon mousse

A mousse like this is very quick and easy to prepare and you can use a wide variety of ripe fruit with a firm but soft texture. Hard fruits like apple and pear can also be used, but these have to be cooked first in a pan with a little water. You may use ready-made custard or vanilla soya dessert instead of cream. If you do, don't add honey.

1 small lemon
1 banana
1/2–1 tablespoon honey
100ml whipping or soya cream

2–3 small portions

Squeeze the lemon. Peel the banana.

Whizz the banana with the honey and half the lemon juice in a blender or food-processor to a fine purée. Add more lemon juice to taste.

Whip the cream and then fold into the banana purée.

Divide the mousse between two or three glasses and serve immediately.

FOR A FAMILY OF FOUR:
MULTIPLY THE INGREDIENTS BY THREE AND SERVE AS A DESSERT.

half-frozen fruit yogurt

You can make this sweet dish up to a day ahead but no earlier. It should then be taken out of the freezer to defrost for at least 30 minutes. If frozen fruits are used for the pureé, the dish can also be served without freezing.

50g fresh or frozen mixed red fruit such as berries or cherries

2 tablespoons 100% fruit strawberry jam

5 tablespoons whipping or soya cream

8 tablespoons live or soya yogurt

2 small portions

Clean the fruit and whizz in a blender or food-processor with the jam to a smooth pureé.

Whip the cream until almost thick and spoon in the yogurt. Add the fruit pureé and fold in gently so that the ingredients do not mix completely.

Divide the mixture between two small bowls or glasses and leave them in the freezer for 1–2 hours.

Tip: Instead of red fruit, try soft orange fruits such as apricots, peaches or mangoes.

FOR A FAMILY OF FOUR:
MULTIPLY THE INGREDIENTS BY FOUR AND SERVE AS A DESSERT.

cauliflower cream with chicken patties

Cauliflower is rich in cancer-fighting nutrients, but it also releases a smell when it is cooked which can make chemo patients feel nauseous. One way to minimise the smell is to put unshelled walnuts or a slice of bread in the cooking water with the cauliflower. Alternatively, bake or steam it. Aluminium and iron pots create a problem too. Cooking cauliflower in an aluminium pot will intensify the unpleasant odour and turn it from creamy white to yellow; iron pots will turn it blue-green or brown.

5 small cauliflower florets
salt and pepper
3 sprigs of fresh parsley
1/2 slice wholemeal bread
50g finely minced chicken
2 tablespoons light cream cheese

2 small portions

Cook the cauliflower in boiling water with a pinch of salt for about 8 minutes until soft. Drain well.

Chop the parsley very finely.

Whizz the bread with the parsley in a blender or food-processor to crumbs. Mix the minced chicken with 2 tablespoons of the breadcrumb mixture, a pinch of salt, a pinch of pepper and a tablespoon of cream cheese. Divide into six portions and shape them into patties.

Place the patties on a steam rack in a pan over boiling water. Cover the pan. Steam for 3–4 minutes until done.

Add the hot cauliflower in the meantime to the rest of the breadcrumbs and whizz to a smooth cream. Add the rest of the parsley and the cream cheese. Season with salt and pepper and reheat.

Put the patties and cauliflower cream in two small bowls.

Tip: The chicken patties have a very soft and delicate texture, but if it is still too difficult to swallow the cooked mince, it may be whizzed in with the cauliflower. The chicken patties can also be cooked on a plate in the microwave; this will take a few minutes on full power.

FOR A FAMILY OF FOUR:
750G CAULIFLOWER, 4 SLICES WHOLEMEAL BREAD, A SMALL BUNCH OF FRESH PARSLEY, 300G FINELY MINCED CHICKEN, 150G LIGHT CREAM CHEESE. MIX THE CHICKEN WITH A QUARTER OF THE BREAD AND THE CREAM CHEESE. SERVE AS A MAIN COURSE.

scrambled egg with ham and chives

How you like your scrambled eggs is very personal. In this recipe it is better not to let them set too much in order to retain the creamy smoothness. Ham and chives can be entirely left out or substituted with smoked salmon and dill.

3 stems of fresh chives
1/2 slice wholemeal bread
1 thin slice ham
2 eggs
2 tablespoons butter
pinch of salt
pinch of pepper

2 small portions

Whizz the bread, the ham and the chives in a blender or food-processor to crumbs.

Beat the eggs a little and pour them into a small saucepan. Add the butter and the breadcrumbs. Cook over a low heat until the eggs have almost set, stirring regularly.

Add a pinch of salt and a pinch of pepper.

Divide between two small plates.

FOR A FAMILY OF FOUR:
MULTIPLY THE INGREDIENTS BY THREE AND SERVE IT FOR BREAKFAST.

bubble and squeak with bacon

This bubble and squeak is mashed very finely but it will still have some texture. For an even smoother result, pulse in a blender or food-processor. Pulsing will ensure that the potatoes don't get sticky and leathery.

about 150g cabbage
2 potatoes
salt and pepper
1 small onion
1 bacon rasher

2 tablespoons olive oil
1½ tablespoons sour or
 soya cream

2 small portions

Wash the cabbage and cut it into small pieces. Peel the potatoes and cut them into 4 pieces. Put them in a small pan with the cabbage and a pinch of salt. Add just enough water to cover the vegetables. Cook for 15–20 minutes until the cabbage is very soft and the potatoes are done. Drain well.

Peel and finely chop the onion in the meantime. Cut the bacon into very small pieces.

Heat the oil in a frying pan and fry the onion and the bacon for 3 minutes over a low heat.

Add the onion and bacon to the strained potatoes and cabbage. Mash or purée on the pulse setting in a blender or food-processor until very fine. Stir in the cream and add salt and pepper to taste.

Divide between two small plates or bowls.

Tip: Adding a small apple (peeled, cored and chopped) to this dish makes a nice change. Add the chopped apple to the pan 10 minutes before the potatoes are done.

FOR A FAMILY OF FOUR:
750G CABBAGE, 1KG POTATOES, 2 BIG ONIONS, 6 BACON RASHERS,
4 TABLESPOONS OLIVE OIL, 6 TABLESPOONS SOUR OR SOYA CREAM. SERVE
AS A MAIN COURSE.

potatoes and broccoli with trout

The smoky flavour of the trout gives this dish an intriguing taste. Other smoked ingredients are suitable too, so you could also use other smoked fish, smoked ham, smoked bacon or smoked sausage.

2 potatoes
salt and pepper
4 small broccoli florets
75g smoked trout fillet
3 stems of fresh chives
2 tablespoons sour or
   soya cream

2 small portions

Peel the potatoes and cut them into four pieces. Put them in a small pan with a pinch of salt. Add just enough water to cover them. Cook for 15–20 minutes until the potatoes are done. Add the broccoli about 5 minutes before the potatoes are done. Drain well.

Chop the trout very finely. Check for bones. Cut the chives very finely.

Mash the potatoes and broccoli very finely or pulse in a blender or food-processor. Add the trout and chives. Stir in the cream. Add salt and pepper to taste.

Tip: You may want to add the trout with the potatoes and broccoli when you purée or mash them together. This way it will get as finely chopped as the rest of the mash.

FOR A FAMILY OF FOUR:
1KG POTATOES, 600G BROCCOLI, 4 SMOKED TROUT FILLETS, SMALL BUNCH OF FRESH CHIVES, 8 TABLESPOONS SOUR OR SOYA CREAM. SERVE AS A MAIN COURSE.

vegetable 'hotchpotch' with cheese

The vegetables can be varied endlessly in this recipe, so you can make all sorts of combinations with your veggie favourites. If the dish is prepared in advance, add the Cheddar after reheating and just before serving. It can also be made without cheese.

6 small carrots
15cm piece of leek
2 potatoes
salt and pepper
1 garlic clove
1 tablespoon olive oil
2 tablespoons light cream cheese
2 tablespoons grated Cheddar
   cheese

2 small portions

Peel and chop the carrots. Wash and finely chop the leek. Peel the potatoes and cut them into 4 pieces.

Put the potatoes in a small pan with the carrots, the leek and a pinch of salt. Add just enough water to cover the vegetables. Cook for 15–20 minutes until the carrots are very soft and the potatoes are done. Drain well.

Peel and chop the garlic. Heat the oil in a small frying pan and fry the garlic for 1 minute.

Add the garlic to the drained potatoes, leek and carrots. Mash very finely, or pulse in a blender or food-processor. Stir in the cream cheese and Cheddar. Add salt and pepper to taste.

Divide between two small plates.

FOR A FAMILY OF FOUR:
500G CARROTS, 4 LEEKS, 1KG POTATOES, 3 GARLIC CLOVES, 2 TABLESPOONS OLIVE OIL, 8 TABLESPOONS LIGHT CREAM CHEESE, 8 TABLESPOONS GRATED CHEDDAR CHEESE. SERVE AS A MAIN COURSE.

experimenting

The recipes in this book are also intended to be a source of inspiration. Use your imagination, your preferred ingredients and your kitchen experience to experiment.

warm pear cream

Try to avoid having too much sugar. If necessary, this cream can be sweetened to taste at the table with a little honey.

2 pear halves, freshly poached
(see tip) or tinned (containing
as little added sugar as
possible)
4 tablespoons crème fraîche or
soya cream
1/2 tablespoon custard powder
1/2 teaspoon ground cinnamon

2 small portions

Whizz the pears in a blender or food-processor to a fine cream. Pass through a sieve. Pour into a small saucepan and add the crème fraîche or cream. Bring to the boil.

Mix the custard powder with a spoonful of liquid from the tinned or poached pears. Stir into the pear mixture and let it thicken over a low heat for a few minutes, stirring every now and then.

Pour into two cups, sprinkle with cinnamon and serve immediately.

Tip: To poach the pears, add 1 teaspoon of honey and a dash of lemon juice to every 100ml of water. Peel and core the pears, and simmer in the poaching liquid for 10–20 minutes until soft.

FOR A FAMILY OF FOUR:
MULTIPLY THE INGREDIENTS BY FOUR AND SERVE AS A DESSERT.

warm or cold?

When asked what he or she would like to eat, a patient will often answer 'something warm' or 'something cold' so you will find both warm and cold recipes in each chapter.

honey custard

This recipe is very simple and just lovely as it is. However, you may choose to add other tasty ingredients such as ground hazelnuts or very finely chopped crystallised ginger in syrup instead of the honey. For a richer custard, you may substitute whipping or soya cream for a quarter of the milk.

250ml skimmed milk or soya milk
2 tablespoons honey
1 tablespoon custard powder

2 small portions

Pour 2 tablespoons of the milk into a cup and set aside. Bring the rest of the milk to the boil with half of the honey.

Mix the custard powder in the cup with the cold milk. Stir into the hot milk and let it thicken. Cook over a low heat for a few minutes, stirring every now and then.

Pour the warm custard into two small bowls and drizzle the remainder of the honey on top.

FOR A FAMILY OF FOUR:
MULTIPLY THE INGREDIENTS BY THREE AND SERVE AS A DESSERT.

warm apricot smoothie

This type of smoothie can be made with all sorts of
purées, using the fruit you have available. It is also
possible to prepare this smoothie with dried apricots,
fresh plums or prunes – just make sure the stones
are out.

10 ripe fresh apricots
250ml skimmed milk or soya milk
1/2 tablespoon honey
100ml live or soya yogurt

2–3 small portions

Wash the apricots and remove the stones.

Bring the milk to the boil with the apricots and honey. Leave to
simmer over a low heat for 5 minutes.

Put the apricots into a blender or food-processor with a little of the
milk and whizz to a smooth purée. Add the rest of the hot milk and
whizz for a further 2 minutes. Add the yogurt.

Pour into two or three glasses or mugs.

FOR A FAMILY OF FOUR:
MULTIPLY THE INGREDIENTS BY FOUR AND SERVE AS A DESSERT.

steamed peach mousse

These mousses are served hot, but you can also let them cool down to serve lukewarm or cold. This will make the texture firmer. Try other fruit like apples or strawberries instead of peaches.

2 peach halves, freshly poached (see tip page 66) or tinned (containing as little added sugar as possible)
2 tablespoons custard powder
2 eggs
3 tablespoons whipping or soya cream
2 tablespoons golden syrup

2–3 small portions

Skin the peach halves if necessary.

Whizz the peaches in a blender or food-processor to a fine purée.

Mix the custard powder with 2 tablespoons of cold water. Whisk together the eggs, custard, cream and syrup until creamy, about 5 minutes. Fold in the peach purée.

Divide between two or three small ramekins. Cover with tin foil. Place on a steaming rack in a pan over boiling water. Cover the pan. Steam for about 10–15 minutes until just set. Remove and then take the foil off.

Place the ramekins on small plates and serve warm.

FOR A FAMILY OF FOUR:
DOUBLE THE INGREDIENTS AND SERVE AS A DESSERT.

eat what you can

What you can and may eat is a personal matter. Healthy food is always preferable, of course. But if it comes down to a choice between eating nothing or something like sugar, it's simple: have sugar and eat!

chapter three

soft with a bite

potato salad

To make this potato salad richer, you could add tiny pieces of ham or chopped cooked prawns.

2 small potatoes
1 carrot
1 spring onion
2 sprigs of fresh parsley
pinch of salt
1 egg
1 tablespoon mayonnaise
pinch of pepper

2 small portions

Peel the potatoes and cut them into small pieces. Peel the carrot, wash the spring onion and chop them both finely. Chop the parsley.

Put the potatoes and the carrot in a pan. Add enough water to cover them and a pinch of salt. Bring the water to a boil and cook for 10–15 minutes or until the potatoes are ready. Add the spring onion and cook for a further 1 minute. Strain and set aside to cool.

Boil the egg for 8 minutes in boiling water. Hold it under cold water until it is cool enough to handle. Remove the shell and chop.

Mix the potatoes, carrot and onion with the egg, half of the parsley and the mayonnaise. Adjust the seasoning.

Serve in two small bowls, sprinkled with the rest of the parsley.

Tip: Other fresh herbs like chives and celery leaf may be used instead or in combination with the parsley.

FOR A FAMILY OF FOUR:
4 EGGS, 8 SMALL POTATOES,
6 CARROTS, 6 SPRING ONIONS,
A SMALL BUNCH OF PARSLEY,
8 TABLESPOONS MAYONNAISE.
SERVE AS A STARTER.

cream cheese and tomato finger sandwiches

It is healthier, if possible, to eat wholemeal bread. It should be soft but not too fresh, as that might make it more difficult to swallow. If the crusts are too hard, just cut them off.

1 ripe tomato
5 stems of fresh chives
2 slices wholemeal bread
1¹/₂ tablespoons light cream cheese

pinch of salt
pinch of pepper

2 small portions

Put the tomato in boiling water for 15 seconds. Rinse under the cold tap and remove the skin. Scoop out the pips, then halve the tomato and cut the flesh into strips.

Chop the chives very finely.

Cut the crusts off the bread if they are too hard.

Spread the slices of bread with the cream cheese.

Put the tomato strips on one slice of bread. Sprinkle with the chives and season with a pinch each of salt and pepper.

Place the other slice of bread cheese-side down on the tomato. Cut the sandwich into fingers and put them on two small plates.

Tip: The tomato may be replaced by avocado or banana. If banana is used, leave out the chives, salt and pepper.

FOR A FAMILY OF FOUR:
MULTIPLY THE INGREDIENTS BY FOUR.

melon and feta salad

To make this recipe work, choose a ripe, sweet melon with a nice aromatic smell. If you cannot find a ripe melon, it's better to use a different fruit, such as a ripe mango or even strawberries. The feta can be left out, and fried bacon bits may be added.

1 spring onion
sprig of fresh parsley
about 25g feta cheese cubes
1 tablespoon lemon juice
2 tablespoons flaxseed or olive oil
pinch of salt
pinch of pepper
1/2 very small cantaloupe melon

2–3 small portions

Wash and chop the spring onion finely. Chop the parsley finely. Crumble the feta cheese.

Mix the spring onion with the parsley, lemon juice, oil, and a pinch each of salt and pepper.

Cut the melon into three wedges and scoop out the seeds. Remove the skin from the melon, cut the flesh into pieces and put them in a bowl.

Mix the feta and spring onion dressing thoroughly with the melon. Place each melon skin wedge on a small plate and spoon over 2–3 good tablespoons of melon salad.

Tip: This melon salad can be kept in the fridge for at least a day, so there is no need to finish it all in one go.

FOR A FAMILY OF FOUR:
DOUBLE THE INGREDIENTS AND SERVE AS A STARTER.

snacks

Recommended 'fast' soft snacks with a bite are shop-bought profiteroles with custard or cream, ripe cherry tomatoes, grapes or cherries and ripe soft fruits. You could also put a lot of different soft fruits together in a delicious fresh fruit salad.

mushroom and tomato pasta salad

The tagliatelle in this recipe can be replaced with any other dried or pre-cooked pasta - just make sure you cook it slightly longer than normal to obtain the recommended soft texture.

2 cherry tomatoes	salt and pepper
6 small mushrooms	2 teaspoons vinegar
2 small broccoli florets	pinch of sugar
2 green beans	
2 sun-dried tomatoes in olive oil	
2 small nests tagliatelle	**2–3 small portions**

Wash the vegetables. Cut the cherry tomatoes, mushrooms, broccoli, beans and sun-dried tomatoes into small pieces.

Cook the tagliatelle in boiling water with a pinch of salt for 2 minutes longer than the suggested time on the packet instructions. Add the pieces of broccoli and beans 5 minutes before the end of the cooking time. Strain.

Heat a small frying pan and add 2 tablespoons of oil from the sun-dried tomatoes. Add the mushrooms and fry for 2 minutes on a low heat. Add the pieces of cherry tomato and sun-dried tomato. Stir in the vinegar, sugar and salt and pepper to taste. Switch off the heat.

Mix all the ingredients together and leave the pasta salad to cool. Serve in two or three small bowls.

Tip: This pasta salad can be kept in the fridge for about a day, so there is no need to finish it all in one go.

FOR A FAMILY OF FOUR:
6 CHERRY TOMATOES, 250G MUSHROOMS, 1 HEAD BROCCOLI, 100G GREEN BEANS, 6 SUN-DRIED TOMATOES, 300G TAGLIATELLE, 6 TABLESPOONS OIL FROM THE SUN-DRIED TOMATOES, 2 TABLESPOONS VINEGAR, SUGAR, SALT AND PEPPER TO TASTE.

aubergine and chicken spread sandwich

This sandwich can also be made with a courgette and it's equally nice with smoked ham or smoked salmon.

1/4 aubergine
1/2 tablespoon olive oil
sprig of fresh parsley
about 25g piece of smoked
    chicken
1 tablespoon light cream
    cheese or fresh cheese

pinch of pepper
1 cherry tomato
4 small lettuce leaves

2 small portions

Wash the aubergine and slice into four rounds. Sprinkle with olive oil and fry in a frying pan until brown on both sides. Set aside to cool.

Chop the parsley.

Whizz the chicken with the cream cheese in a blender or food-processor until smooth. Add a pinch of pepper and the parsley.

Cut the cherry tomato into six tiny wedges.

Spoon a teaspoon of chicken spread on to a slice of aubergine. Wash the lettuce leaves and then put two of them, half the remaining chicken spread and half the tomato wedges on top. Cover with a second aubergine slice and repeat with the remaining ingredients.

Serve on two small plates.

Tip: The aubergine may be peeled and the tomato skinned, if necessary.

FOR A FAMILY OF FOUR:
DOUBLE THE INGREDIENTS AND SERVE AS A STARTER.

quick custard and raspberry ice cream

You can buy the custard for this recipe ready-made. If you would rather make your own custard from a packet, there's no need to add sugar for sweetness – a tiny little bit of honey will do. Make sure you let the custard get cold first before mixing it in.

150g frozen raspberries
150ml ready-made custard
1–2 tablespoons raspberry syrup

2 small portions

Whizz the raspberries in a blender or food-processor. Make sure the mixture is as fine as possible but still frozen.

Mix in the custard and the syrup to taste.

Spoon into two glasses or bowls and serve immediately.

Tip: You could use blackberries instead of raspberries.

FOR A FAMILY OF FOUR:
MULTIPLY THE INGREDIENTS BY THREE AND SERVE AS A DESSERT.

choose untreated

Weedkillers and insecticides have adverse effects on the immune system. It's therefore always best to choose untreated (ecological) ingredients. Always wash fruit and vegetables well whether organic or not to kill *E. coli* bacteria.

berry jelly

To make sure you get as many vitamins as possible, the whole fruit is used for this jelly. As a result, the jelly is not as clear as one made from a packet.

200g strawberries
150g blueberries
5g gelatine powder or 3
    gelatine leaves
1 tablespoon honey

2–3 small portions

Wash the fruit. Set aside a strawberry and two blueberries.

Whizz the remaining strawberries and blueberries in a blender or food-processor. Make sure the mixture is as fine as possible and pass through a sieve.

Prepare or soak the gelatine according to the instructions on the packet.

Put a quarter of the fruit purée into a small saucepan with the honey. Bring to the boil, then remove the pan from the heat. Stir in the gelatine and let it dissolve, then stir in the rest of the fruit purée. Pour into two or three glasses.

Leave in the fridge to set for at least 2 hours.

Cut the strawberry set aside into four wedges. Garnish the jelly with strawberry wedges and blueberries.

Tip: This type of jelly can also be made with a single ripe fruit or other combinations. Try mangoes, melons, peaches, nectarines, apricots, plums, grapes, cherries, redcurrants and other berries.

FOR A FAMILY OF FOUR:
MULTIPLY THE INGREDIENTS BY FOUR AND SERVE AS A DESSERT.

creamy rice pudding with cranberries

As with most recipes, this rice pudding is sweetened with honey because that is considered healthier than white sugar.

200ml skimmed or soya milk
2 tablespoons easy-cook
    dessert rice
2 tablespoons half-dried
    cranberries

1–1½ tablespoons honey
7½ tablespoons whipping or
    soya cream

2–3 small portions

Bring the milk to a boil in a small saucepan with the rice, cranberries and honey to taste. Turn down the heat as low as possible and let it simmer until the rice is soft, stirring occasionally. The cooking time varies with the brand and will be stated on the packet.

Set aside to cool, stirring occasionally.

Whip the cream until almost stiff and fold into the cold rice pudding.

Divide between two or three small bowls or glasses.

Tip: The cranberries can be replaced by other dried fruits like apples, prunes, figs, apricots or raisins.

FOR A FAMILY OF FOUR:
MULTIPLY THE INGREDIENTS BY THREE AND SERVE AS A DESSERT.

honeyed fruit salad

This fruit salad is served with a lemon and honey dressing. For some people, it may be a bit too acidic. If that's the case, use a bottled fruit syrup instead.

¹/₂ small lemon
¹/₂ tablespoon honey
1 banana
1 peach or nectarine, fresh or tinned
  (containing as little added sugar as
  possible)
1 kiwi fruit

2-3 small portions

Squeeze the lemon juice into a big bowl. Add the honey and stir until it has dissolved.

Peel the banana. Remove the skin from the peach and the kiwi fruit. Halve the peach and take out the stone.

Cut the fruit into small pieces and mix them with the honey mixture. Leave for at least 10 minutes.

Divide between two or three glasses or bowls.

Tip: Most fruits can easily be mixed with others. It is best to use ripe soft fruits when they are in season.

FOR A FAMILY OF FOUR:
MULTIPLY THE INGREDIENTS BY THREE AND SERVE AS A DESSERT.

mint and ginger

Some natural ingredients have medicinal properties that ease nausea and stomach ache. In mild cases, try some mint tea or fresh ginger (used in dishes or in ginger tea) – they will offer some relief.

chicken ragout

Ragouts are nice and smooth and often go down well. The chicken in this recipe can be replaced with a good, fresh ham without preservatives from your local butcher, cooked fish or prawns. If you use fish or prawns, you may want to use fish stock.

10 tablespoons easy-cook whole grain
   rice
2 runner beans
⅛ red pepper
2 spring onions
pinch of salt
50g cooked or smoked chicken
1 tablespoon olive oil
1 small tablespoon flour
200ml chicken stock made with a stock
   cube or home-made
2 tablespoons crème fraîche
   or soya cream
pinch of pepper

2 small portions

Cook the rice in boiling water following the instructions on the packet. Drain.

Wash the beans and slice them very thinly. Wash and deseed the red pepper. Wash the spring onions and chop into very small pieces.

Cook the beans and red pepper for 8 minutes in boiling water with a pinch of salt. Add the spring onions after 5 minutes and cook together for a further 3 minutes. Drain.

Cut the chicken into small pieces.

Heat the olive oil in a saucepan. Take it off the heat and stir in the flour. Heat for 3 minutes, stirring occasionally. Take it off the heat again and stir in half of the stock. Bring to the boil, stirring continuously, adding more stock when the sauce gets thicker. When all the stock is stirred in, add the vegetables and the chicken.

Stir in the crème fraîche or cream and let it cook on a low heat for a few minutes. Season.

Serve the rice with the ragout on two small plates.

Tip: Rice is not easy to eat for everyone who is ill. It can be replaced by pasta or potatoes.

FOR A FAMILY OF FOUR:
300G EASY-COOK WHOLE GRAIN RICE, 400G RUNNER BEANS, 2 RED PEPPERS, 8 SPRING ONIONS, 300G COOKED OR SMOKED CHICKEN, 6 TABLESPOONS OLIVE OIL, 3 TABLESPOONS FLOUR, 1 LITRE CHICKEN STOCK, 8 TABLESPOONS CRÈME FRAÎCHE, SALT AND PEPPER TO TASTE.

onion sizes

The ingredients lists in this book frequently include 'a small onion'. This refers to an onion of about 30–40 grams. Spring onions should weigh about 20 grams.

macaroni with leek, ham and cheese

This macaroni can be finished in the oven or under the grill, with some extra cheese 'au gratin' on top. Don't let it get too crispy, though, since that might make it hard to swallow.

about 50g macaroni
about 10cm piece of leek
1 small tomato
about 30g slice fresh ham without
    preservatives, from the butcher
2 sprigs of fresh parsley
2 tablespoons olive oil
2 tablespoons light cream cheese
2 tablespoons grated Cheddar cheese
pinch of salt
pinch of pepper

2 small portions

Cook the macaroni in boiling water following the packet instructions. Drain.

Wash the leek and cut into very thin slices. Wash the tomato and cut into small pieces. Cut the ham into fine strips. Chop the parsley.

Heat the olive oil in saucepan and fry the leek for 3 minutes over a medium heat. Add the tomato and fry for a further 1 minute.

Add the cream cheese and let it melt. Stir in the grated Cheddar and heat until melted. Add the macaroni, ham, half the parsley and season to taste with a pinch each of salt and pepper. Heat for a further 1 minute.

Serve on two small plates and sprinkle with the rest of the parsley.

Tip: Leeks taste not only great, but also provide some extra colour to the dish, which helps in the appreciation of the food. If there are no leeks available, onions can be used instead.

FOR A FAMILY OF FOUR:
300G MACARONI, 3 LEEKS, 6 TOMATOES, 200G HAM, A SMALL BUNCH OF PARSLEY, 4 TABLESPOONS OLIVE OIL, 200G LIGHT CREAM CHEESE, 8 TABLESPOONS GRATED CHEDDAR CHEESE, SALT AND PEPPER TO TASTE.

oriental rice with fruit and nuts

The flavour of this aromatic, sweet and savoury rice may be enriched by adding a thread of saffron (soaked in a teaspoon of hot water). A cardamom seed can also be used. Both ingredients should be put in at the same time as the dried fruits.

1 orange
1 tablespoon honey
2 pieces dried apricot
2 pieces prune
2 pieces dried apple
about 10cm piece of leek
4 tablespoons mixed nuts (but not peanuts)

10 tablespoons easy-cook whole grain rice
1 tablespoon olive oil
1/2 vegetable stock cube
1 teaspoon cinnamon

2 small portions

Wash the orange and grate the zest coarsely into a small saucepan. Halve and squeeze all of the orange juice into the pan. Add the honey and cook for 2 minutes on a medium heat. Set aside to cool.

Chop the dried fruits, leek and nuts finely. Wash the rice.

Heat the olive oil in a small saucepan. Fry the leek for 3 minutes over a low heat. Stir in the rice, fruits, nuts, 300ml water and the stock cube.

Cook the rice over a very low heat until dry and soft (according to the packet instructions). If the rice is dry but not yet soft, add a little more hot water and cook until done.

Mix in the cinnamon. Serve the rice on two small plates and add the orange and honey syrup to taste.

Tip: Since it spoils easily, reheating cooked rice is not recommended so it's better to make just enough and eat it when fresh.

FOR A FAMILY OF FOUR:
2 ORANGES, 2 TABLESPOONS HONEY, 150G DRIED FRUITS, 2 LEEKS, 12 TABLESPOONS NUTS, 350G EASY-COOK WHOLE GRAIN RICE, 3 TABLESPOONS OLIVE OIL, 1 1/2 STOCK CUBES, 1 1/2 LITRES WATER, 4 TEASPOONS CINNAMON.

stir-fried chicken noodles

For this dish you can choose between egg noodles, rice noodles and special stir-fry noodles. You can easily change the vegetables and chicken to whatever mix you prefer. To make it a vegetarian meal, replace the chicken with pieces of omelette or tofu.

about 50g noodles
1 small lemon
4 spring onions
¼ red pepper
6 shiitake mushrooms
about 50g piece chicken breast

1 tablespoon olive oil
1 tablespoon sweet thick soy
  sauce
salt and pepper

2–3 small portions

Cook the noodles in boiling water for 1 minute longer than the suggested time on the packet instructions. Strain and set aside to cool.

Wash the lemon and grate the zest coarsely (you will need 2 small teaspoons of zest). Halve the lemon.

Wash the spring onions and red pepper and wipe the mushrooms. Deseed the red pepper and chop all the vegetables into small pieces.

Cut the chicken into small strips.

Heat the oil in a wok. Add the chicken and stir-fry on a low heat for 3 minutes. Add the vegetables and stir-fry for a further 5 minutes. Mix in the noodles and the lemon zest and stir-fry a little bit longer until the noodles are hot. Add the soy sauce and squeeze a little bit of lemon juice over the dish. Season.

Serve the noodles in two or three small bowls. A wedge of lemon may be added.

Tip: Cooked noodles can be kept in the fridge for about a day. However, they are at their best when freshly cooked.

FOR A FAMILY OF FOUR:
300G NOODLES, ZEST AND JUICE OF 1 LEMON, 8 SPRING ONIONS, 2 RED PEPPERS, 250G SHIITAKE MUSHROOMS, 200G CHICKEN BREAST, 2 TABLESPOONS OLIVE OIL, SWEET, THICK SOY SAUCE TO TASTE.

grilled pepper and cheese pancakes

These pancakes can also be served with a choice of sweet toppings but to do so, you may want to add some vanilla sugar to the batter.

4 tablespoons wholemeal flour
pinch of salt
100ml skimmed or soya milk
3 tablespoons beaten egg
1 grilled pepper from a jar
sprig of fresh parsley
splash of olive oil

2 tablespoons tomato ketchup
  or tomato sauce
3 tablespoons grated Cheddar
  cheese

2 small portions

Mix the flour, a pinch of salt, milk and egg together and whisk until the batter is smooth.

Cut the pepper into strips. Chop the parsley.

Heat a splash of olive oil in a big frying pan. Place two spoonfuls of batter next to each other in the pan and fry the pancakes for a few minutes until dry on top and light brown on the other side. Flip them over and spread with the tomato ketchup or sauce.

Place the pepper strips on top and sprinkle with the grated cheese. Fry for a further minute on a low heat until the cheese has melted.

Place the pancakes on two small plates and sprinkle with the parsley.

Tip: If you cannot or do not want to eat Cheddar cheese, you don't have to use it. You can use light cream cheese instead.

FOR A FAMILY OF FOUR:
MULTIPLY THE INGREDIENTS BY FOUR AND SERVE FOR LUNCH.

porridge with almonds and honey

The right thickness of porridge is a matter of personal preference. In order to make it thicker or thinner, you simply add more or less oats. Should it still be too thick, just add some more milk and heat the porridge a while longer.

250ml skimmed or soya milk
5 tablespoons porridge oats
pinch of salt
2 tablespoons ground almonds
1–2 tablespoons honey
2 tablespoons whipping or
    soya cream

2 small portions

Bring the milk, oats, a pinch of salt and the almonds slowly to a boil on a medium heat. Keep stirring until the porridge starts to get thick and creamy, then turn down the heat and let the porridge cook for a further few minutes.

Divide the porridge between two bowls and top with the honey and cream. Stir a bit before serving.

Tip: As a welcome variation, the porridge can be sweetened with all sorts of ingredients such as 100% fruit jam or fresh sweet fruit.

FOR A FAMILY OF FOUR:
MULTIPLY THE INGREDIENTS BY FOUR.

textures to suit the situation

Patients may prefer different textures during the various stages of chemotherapy, depending on the effects of their treatment at any particular time. This might mean that sometimes they can enjoy any of the textures here, while at other times, perhaps only one certain texture will appeal.

fried banana and maple cream

This is a recipe for one of those days when you don't feel like being good and you want to indulge yourself. Use pineapple or apple as an alternative to the banana if you wish. Even after cooking, the texture of pineapple is not as soft as that of banana, so only choose this variation if it is possible for the patient to swallow firm textures.

7 tablespoons whipping cream
4 tablespoons maple syrup
1 banana
1 tablespoon butter

2 small portions

Whip the cream with 1 tablespoon of maple syrup until almost stiff.

Peel the banana and cut into thick slices.

Melt the butter in a frying pan and cook the slices of banana for 1–2 minutes on each side until brown. Add the rest of the maple syrup and heat for a further 1/2 minute.

Place the banana slices in two small bowls and spoon over some maple cream and the hot maple syrup from the pan.

Tip: In this book, olive oil is usually recommended for frying instead of butter. However, in this recipe butter is the preference.

FOR A FAMILY OF FOUR:
MULTIPLY THE INGREDIENTS BY FOUR AND SERVE AS A DESSERT.

jam crêpes with vanilla sugar

For this recipe it is best to use jam made with 100% fruit. If not available, any other jam can be used provided it is very low in sugar.

2 tablespoons wholemeal flour
1/2 tablespoon vanilla sugar
pinch of salt
6 tablespoons skimmed or
    soya milk
1 tablespoon whisked egg
splash of mild olive oil
2 tablespoons 100% fruit jam
1 teaspoon icing sugar

2 small portions

Mix the flour, vanilla sugar, salt, milk and egg together and stir until the batter is smooth.

Heat a splash of olive oil in a small frying pan. Pour half of the batter into the pan and fry the crêpe for a few minutes until dry on top and light brown on the other side.

Flip over and fry for a further minute or so until light brown. Slide on to a plate and repeat with the remaining batter to make a second crêpe.

Place the crêpes on two small plates. Spread with the jam, roll up and dust with the icing sugar.

Tip: These crêpes may be served with a scoop of ice cream or some fresh fruit.

FOR A FAMILY OF FOUR:
MULTIPLY THE INGREDIENTS BY SIX AND SERVE AS A DESSERT.

stewed fruit with ice cream

Since dried fruits keep so well, they are ideal to have to hand so that you can quickly prepare a dish when it's needed. However, you can also use fresh fruit if you have it for this recipe – just make sure that you wash them before you use them.

2 prunes
2 ready-to-eat dried apricots
1 tablespoon dried cranberries
   or raisins
1/2 lemon
1/2–1 tablespoon honey
1 teaspoon arrowroot
2 scoops ice cream

2 small portions

Cut the prunes, apricots and cranberries into pieces.

Squeeze the juice from the lemon into a saucepan. Add 100ml water and honey to taste and bring to the boil. Stir until the honey is dissolved. Add the prunes, apricots and cranberries or raisins and cook for 5 minutes over a low heat.

Mix the arrowroot with 1/2 a tablespoon of cold water and stir it into the fruit mixture. Cook for 2 minutes.

Scoop the ice cream on to two small dishes and spoon the warm fruit stew next to it.

FOR A FAMILY OF FOUR:
MULTIPLY THE INGREDIENTS BY FOUR AND SERVE AS A DESSERT.

a little at a time
Big portions of food can easily put patients off, so it's better to serve several small portions of food at different times throughout the day.

chapter four

liquid

chilled carrot and citrus soup

This smooth and creamy soup can be made thinner or thicker to your liking. Just add more or less stock. Like most cold soups, it can also be served warm.

1/2 slice wholemeal bread
4 carrots
1 small onion
1 small lemon
1 small orange
2 stems of fresh chives
(optional)
3 tablespoons olive oil

150ml low fat chicken
stock from a cube or
home-made
5 tablespoons whipping or
soya cream
salt and pepper

2 small portions

Cut off the crusts and cut the bread in cubes. Peel and chop the carrots and onion. Wash and zest the lemon. Squeeze the juice out of half the lemon and all of the orange. Wash and chop the chives finely.

Heat the olive oil in a saucepan. Add the carrots, the onion and the lemon zest. Fry for 3 minutes over a medium heat. Add the bread cubes, 1/2 tablespoon of lemon juice, the orange juice and the stock. Cook for 10–15 minutes until the carrots are very soft. Add the cream and cook for a further minute.

Whizz in a blender or food-processor. Make sure the soup is completely smooth. Add salt and pepper to taste and leave to cool. Keep the soup in the fridge until needed.

Pour into two glasses or bowls and sprinkle with chives, if using, and some extra lemon zest.

Tip: For this recipe it is also very nice to use pumpkin or courgette instead of carrots.

FOR A FAMILY OF FOUR:
MULTIPLY THE INGREDIENTS BY THREE AND SERVE AS A STARTER.

cucumber and apple smoothie

This smoothie can be made with all sorts of fruit juice. The yogurt can also be omitted and replaced by a similar amount of fruit juice.

1/2 cucumber
1/4 slice wholemeal bread
2 fresh mint leaves
150ml live or soya yogurt

100ml apple juice
pinch of salt
pinch of pepper

2 small portions

Peel and chop the cucumber. Cut off the crusts and cut the bread into pieces.

Whizz all the ingredients in a blender or food-processor. Make sure the mixture is as smooth as possible.

Pour into two glasses and serve immediately or leave it in the fridge until needed.

Tip: 1/2 tablespoon of honey can be added to sweeten this smoothie. However, it is better to avoid the sugar, if you can resist it.

FOR A FAMILY OF FOUR:
MULTIPLY THE INGREDIENTS BY THREE AND SERVE AS A DRINK.

savoury raspberry gazpacho

Traditionally, this cold soup is prepared with tomatoes (very nice and highly recommended) but this variation with raspberries is even more appreciated by both sick people and their family members. Variations on this gazpacho can also be made with strawberries, blackberries or blueberries.

1/2 cucumber
1/2 shallot or small onion
1 small garlic clove
1/4 slice wholemeal bread
5 tablespoons olive oil
1-2 teaspoons raspberry or
    balsamic vinegar
150g frozen or fresh raspberries
salt and pepper
1/2-1 tablespoon raspberry syrup

2 small portions

Peel the cucumber, the shallot or onion and the garlic. Cut off the crusts and cut the bread into cubes.

Whizz all the ingredients except for 2 raspberries and the seasonings in a blender or food-processor with 3 tablespoons of cold water. Make sure the mixture is as smooth as possible. Season with salt and pepper and add raspberry syrup to taste.

Pour into two glasses or bowls, put a raspberry in the middle and serve immediately or leave in the fridge until needed.

Tip: Adding a dash of Tabasco is very nice but could be too strong. Therefore it's best to let those who like spicy food add Tabasco themselves, to taste.

FOR A FAMILY OF FOUR:
DOUBLE THE INGREDIENTS AND SERVE AS A STARTER.

snacks

Recommended ready-to-eat liquid snacks are tomato or mixed vegetable juice (especially carrot juice which is excellent), fruit juices, breakfast drinks and smoothies. Look out for juices without added sugar; you can always spice them up at home if necessary.

chilled tomato and red pepper soup

A quick and easy cold soup that doesn't need any cooking. It can also be served hot.

¹/₂ slice wholemeal bread
2 grilled red peppers from a jar
sprig of fresh parsley or a few
   fresh basil leaves
250ml tomato juice
2 tablespoons olive oil
salt and pepper

2 small portions

Cut off the crusts and cut the bread into cubes.

Whizz all the ingredients in a blender or food-processor. Make sure the mixture is as smooth as possible.

Pour into two glasses or bowls. Serve immediately or leave in the fridge until needed.

Tip: Red peppers in a jar often taste very nice and a little of the liquid can be added to the soup to enhance the flavour. If you prefer to grill the peppers yourself, you'll find instructions on page 38.

FOR A FAMILY OF FOUR:
MULTIPLY THE INGREDIENTS BY THREE AND SERVE AS A STARTER.

spinach and walnut smoothie

Smoothies can be made with vegetables or fruit or a mixture of both – the possibilities are endless. And since they are nutritious as well as quick and easy to prepare, they're ideal as an 'instant' liquid meal. They are usually made with milk, buttermilk or yogurt, but if dairy products don't go down well, try puréed avocado, tomato juice or carrot juice instead.

50g fresh spinach
2 tablespoons shelled walnuts
250ml buttermilk

$1/2$–1 tablespoon honey
salt and pepper

2–3 small portions

Wash and dry the spinach thoroughly.

Whizz the spinach, walnuts, buttermilk and honey in a blender or food-processor. Make sure the mixture is as smooth as possible. Season.

Pour into two or three glasses and serve immediately or leave in the fridge until needed.

Tip: In this recipe, fresh spinach can be replaced with frozen spinach. Let it defrost first or, for a really cold smoothie, whizz it 10 minutes after you've taken it out of the freezer.

FOR A FAMILY OF FOUR:
MULTIPLY THE INGREDIENTS BY THREE
AND SERVE AS A DRINK.

almond and peach smoothie

Soft fruits such as peaches are ideal for smoothies like this one. However, the fruits must be ripe. The same goes for apricots, plums, melon, mango, bananas, and all sorts of berries.

2 ripe peaches
5 tablespoons peach syrup
4 tablespoons ground almonds
200ml skimmed or soya milk

2 small portions

Peel, half and stone the peaches.

Whizz all the ingredients in a blender or food-processor. Make sure the mixture is as smooth as possible.

Pour into glasses and serve immediately or leave it in the fridge until needed.

Tip: This smoothie can also be made with tinned peaches, using the syrup from the tin. If milk is a problem, replace it with fruit juice.

FOR A FAMILY OF FOUR:
MULTIPLY THE INGREDIENTS BY THREE AND SERVE AS A DRINK.

the challenge

Cooking for somebody with cancer can be very rewarding but also very disappointing. All you want is the patient to appreciate the food, eat well and keep strong. However, it could easily be that the patient can't eat any of the dishes you have so carefully prepared. Unfortunately this is just part of the reality. Try to accept it with as light a spirit as possible because it is frustrating not only for the cook but also for the patient.

ice-cold strawberry and cranberry juice

The strawberries used in this recipe are frozen. Take them out of the freezer 10 minutes before use so they will be easier to purée.

250g frozen strawberries
5 tablespoons sugar-free
   cranberry juice

2 small portions

Whizz the strawberries in a blender or food-processor to a very fine purée. Add the cranberry juice. Whizz for a further minute.

Pour into two glasses and serve immediately.

Tip: To sweeten this cold juice, some honey may be added.

FOR A FAMILY OF FOUR:
MULTIPLY THE INGREDIENTS BY THREE AND SERVE AS A DRINK.

chilled mixed fruit soup

You could replace the melon, tangerine and kiwi fruit with all sorts of different fruity combinations. Some ideas include melon, plums and raspberries; banana, kiwi and mango; nectarine, red currants and passion fruit or pear, blackberries and orange.

1 small wedge of ripe melon
2 tangerines
1 ripe kiwi fruit
1 tablespoon honey

1–2 small portions

Peel the fruit.

Whizz all the ingredients in a blender or food-processor. Make sure the mixture is as smooth as possible.

Strain the juice.

Pour into one or two small bowls and serve immediately or leave in the fridge until needed.

Tip: This fruit soup can be diluted by adding some fruit juice, to taste.

FOR A FAMILY OF FOUR:
MULTIPLY THE INGREDIENTS BY FOUR AND SERVE AS A DESSERT.

make it special

Try to treat eating as a social event, especially when the chemotherapy is having side effects and patients are feeling less and less like eating. This will hopefully encourage them to eat more. Always prepare at least two portions. The extra portion can be kept in the fridge for at least another day, to be eaten at a convenient time.

banana and ginger milkshake

Milkshakes are delicious, creamy and cold and often go down easily. However, since they contain milk, ice cream or dairy products, they may cause problems. If so, use fruit juice and sorbet instead of milk and ice cream.

1 banana
about 10g fresh ginger
4 tablespoons ginger syrup
1 tablespoon fresh lime juice
3 scoops of vanilla ice cream
100ml skimmed or soya milk

2 small portions

Peel the banana and ginger. Grate the ginger finely.

Whizz the banana with the grated ginger, the ginger syrup and the lime juice to a very smooth purée in a blender or food-processor.

Add the ice cream and milk and whizz for a few more minutes.

Pour into two glasses and serve immediately.

Tip: For a comparable milkshake, all types of soft fruits may be used. Lime juice can be replaced by lemon or orange juice and ginger syrup by any 100% fruit jam. Fresh ginger can be left out, so this is a very flexible recipe.

FOR A FAMILY OF FOUR:
MULTIPLY THE INGREDIENTS BY THREE.

be flexible

Since appetite may come and go within minutes, try not to be disappointed or too pushy if the food you have prepared is rejected.

fennel soup with cream

This soup is best when very smooth and creamy. If it isn't as smooth as you expected, it can be strained before serving. The bread used in creamy soups can be left out if the patient cannot tolerate it.

1/2 slice wholemeal bread
1 fennel bulb
1 small onion
3 tablespoons olive oil
250ml chicken stock from a stock cube or home-made
5 tablespoons whipping or soya cream
salt and pepper

2 small portions

Cut off the crusts and cut the bread into cubes. Wash and chop the fennel, then set the fronds aside. Peel and chop the onion.

Heat the olive oil in a saucepan. Add the fennel and the onion and fry for 3 minutes over a medium heat. Add the bread and the stock. Cook until the fennel is very soft, 15–20 minutes. Add the cream and cook for 1 minute.

Whizz to a smooth soup in a blender or food-processor. Add salt and pepper to taste.

Ladle into two bowls and sprinkle with the fennel fronds.

Tip: This recipe is also delicious with celery or cucumber instead of fennel.

FOR A FAMILY OF FOUR:
DOUBLE THE INGREDIENTS AND SERVE AS A STARTER.

wholemeal wheat

Wholemeal bread is used a lot in the recipes. Among other things, it helps the digestive system. However, it will not necessarily be good for everybody. With people suffering from intestine or stomach problems it might trigger cramps, as wholemeal is more difficult to digest. If so, use white bread instead. If that causes digestive problems too, you can leave the bread out of most recipes.

chicken and tomato broth

This soup can be made either with stock cubes or home-made chicken stock. The latter option will take longer to cook, but it is preferable. However the smell of fresh chicken stock might be off-putting to some patients.

1 small onion
2 carrots
2 celery stalks
2 ripe tomatoes
1 chicken leg or 2 chicken
stock cubes

1 blade of mace
1 bay leaf
sprig of fresh thyme
salt and pepper

6–8 small portions

Peel and chop the onion and the carrots. Wash and chop the celery and tomatoes.

Bring 800ml water to a boil with the chicken leg or stock cubes. While the chicken is cooking, skim the broth. If using cubes, stir until they are dissolved.

Add the vegetables, the spices, the herbs and a pinch each of salt and pepper. Leave to simmer on a low heat. If using stock cubes, simmer for 30 minutes; if using the chicken leg, simmer for 2 hours.

Strain the stock, reserving the vegetables and the chicken, and season to taste.

Serve in small bowls. Some of the cooked vegetables and a few small pieces of the chicken can be added, depending on how difficult it is for the patient to swallow.

Keep the remainder of the soup in the fridge or freezer.

FOR A FAMILY OF FOUR:
SERVE AS A STARTER.

cream of aubergine and tomato soup

When prepared without stock, this recipe can be turned into a lovely purée to be enjoyed on its own or on a slice of soft bread.

1/2 slice wholemeal bread
1/4 aubergine
1 small tomato
2 spring onions
1 garlic clove
3 tablespoons olive oil

pinch of ground cumin
200ml vegetable stock from a
 stock cube or home-made
salt and pepper

2–3 small portions

Cut off the crusts and cut the bread into cubes. Wash and chop the aubergine, tomato and spring onions. Peel and chop the garlic.

Heat the olive oil in a saucepan. Add the aubergine, tomato, spring onions and garlic. Fry for 3 minutes over a medium heat. Add a pinch of ground cumin, the bread and the stock. Cook until the aubergine is very soft, 10–15 minutes.

Whizz to a very smooth soup in a blender or food-processor. Season to taste.

Pour into small bowls.

Tip: If it appeals to the patient, you could reserve a tablespoon of spring onion to sprinkle over the soup just before serving.

FOR A FAMILY OF FOUR:
MULTIPLY THE INGREDIENTS BY FOUR AND SERVE AS A STARTER.

vegetable soup

It's best to make this soup in large quantities and then keep it in the fridge for a few days. It can also be frozen, preferably in small portions, so it is easy to defrost just what you need.

1 small carrot	3 sprigs of fresh parsley
1/4 leek	1 vegetable stock cube
1 celery stalk	salt and pepper
4 button or shiitake mushrooms	
1 tomato	**3–4 small portions**

Peel, wash and then cut all the vegetables and herbs very finely (this is easily done in a food processor).

Bring 400ml water to the boil with the stock cube and the vegetables. Simmer for 15–30 minutes. The longer they cook, the softer the vegetables will be.

Add salt and pepper to taste.

Serve in small bowls. Keep the rest of the soup in the fridge or freeze it.

Tip: This vegetable soup may also be puréed and all sorts of herbs and spices can be added to taste: try curry powder, paprika, thyme, chives or dill.

FOR A FAMILY OF FOUR:
DOUBLE THE INGREDIENTS AND SERVE AS A STARTER.

pumpkin soup with soy sauce

Pumpkin has a sweet taste and when cooked it has a very soft texture. It's lovely as a base for soups. It can be replaced by other soft vegetables such as aubergine, sweet potato, courgette or asparagus.

½ slice wholemeal bread
about 150g wedge of pumpkin
1 small onion
1 garlic clove
sprig of fresh parsley or coriander
3 tablespoons olive oil

pinch of curry powder
250ml chicken stock from a
    stock cube or home-made
splash of soy sauce
2 small portions

Cut off the crusts and cut the bread into cubes. Peel and chop the pumpkin, onion and garlic. Chop the parsley or coriander finely.

Heat the olive oil in a saucepan. Add the pumpkin, the onion and the garlic. Fry for 3 minutes over a medium heat. Add a pinch of curry powder, the bread and the stock. Cook until the pumpkin is very soft, about 10–15 minutes.

Whizz to a very smooth soup in a blender or food-processor. Add soy sauce to taste.

Pour into two small bowls and sprinkle with the parsley or coriander.

Tip: Some spiciness, such as Tabasco, and acidity, such as lemon or lime juice, can be added at the table according to personal taste.

FOR A FAMILY OF FOUR:
MULTIPLY THE INGREDIENTS BY FOUR AND SERVE AS A STARTER.

indian tea with milk and spices

This aromatic tea is normally served hot or warm. However it is also very nice to serve it chilled.

200ml skimmed or soya milk
1 bay leaf
2 cardamom seeds
1 tablespoon green tea leaves
honey to taste

2 small portions

Bring the milk to a boil with 100ml water, the bay leaf and the cardamom seeds. Let it simmer for 5 minutes.

Turn off the heat. Add the tea leaves and leave to steep for 5 minutes.

Strain the tea into two glasses or cups. Add honey to taste.

FOR A FAMILY OF FOUR:
MULTIPLY THE INGREDIENTS BY FOUR.

flavourings

Adding herbs and spices is a touchy subject. You will have to find out by trial and error how much salt, pepper, herbs, spices and honey is enjoyable for the patient. It's much easier to add a few extra flavourings at the table than having to make a dish, which is too strongly flavoured, milder.

hot aniseed milk

Milk is not always easy to drink, but served warm it often feels good. The milk in this recipe can be replaced by tea.

250ml skimmed or soya milk
$1/2$ teaspoon grated orange zest
2 tablespoons aniseed
$1/2$-1 tablespoon honey

2 small portions

Heat the milk for 10 minutes with the orange zest, the aniseed and honey to taste. Don't let it boil. Whisk well.

Strain into two cups or heatproof glasses.

Tip: Only the orange zest is used in this recipe. The rest of the orange can be kept in the fridge for a day or so until needed.

FOR A FAMILY OF FOUR:
MULTIPLY THE INGREDIENTS BY THREE.

very fine food
Dishes can always be made finer, by rubbing them carefully through a sieve.

honey and pear soup

Sweet fruit soups normally need a little bit of acidity for a proper balance in taste. As the experience of taste alters so much during treatment it may be necessary to fine-tune the sour and sweet components.

$1/2$ slice wholemeal bread
1 ripe pear
1 small lemon
$1/2$-1 tablespoon honey
100ml whipping or soya cream

2 small portions

Cut off the crusts and cut the bread into cubes.

Peel, core and quarter the pear. Wash and zest the lemon. Juice half of the lemon.

Bring $3/4$ of the lemon juice to a boil with the zest, the bread, the pear quarters and honey to taste. Cook for 10 minutes, stirring regularly.

Whizz in a blender or food-processor to a smooth purée. Add the cream. Cook for a further 1 minute. Add more lemon juice to taste.

Pour into two small bowls.

Tip: As an alternative you could use apple, peach or mango.

FOR A FAMILY OF FOUR:
MULTIPLY THE INGREDIENTS BY THREE AND SERVE AS A DESSERT.

warm apple juice with cinnamon

For this recipe, it's best to use a juicer. This kitchen tool makes it very easy to prepare fresh fruit and vegetable juices in a matter of minutes.

3 sweet and juicy apples
1 teaspoon honey
1 cinnamon stick

2 small portions

Wash the apples. Juice them in a juicer.

Bring the juice to the boil with the honey and cinnamon stick. Let it simmer for 5 minutes, then remove the cinnamon stick. Stir well for 1 minute.

Pour the warm juice into two heatproof glasses or cups.

Tip: If you don't have a juicer, you could use natural apple juice.

FOR A FAMILY OF FOUR:
MULTIPLY THE INGREDIENTS BY FOUR.

chapter five

crispy

potato 'cookies' with egg salad

If you think the taste of spring onions will be too strong in this recipe, replace them with fresh chives. These 'cookies' are also very nice with other salads or with smoked fish, prawns or thinly sliced meats.

1 egg
2 small spring onions
3 sprigs of fresh parsley
1 tablespoon mayonnaise
pinch of salt

pinch of pepper
1 small potato
splash of olive oil

2 small portions

Boil the egg for 8 minutes, then hold it under cold running water and let it cool.

Chop the spring onions and parsley. Shell the egg. Chop it and mix it with 3/4 of the spring onion, 3/4 of the parsley, the mayonnaise, a pinch each of salt and pepper.

Peel the potato and grate it on a fine grater but don't rinse it afterwards. Mix with a pinch each of salt and pepper. Put it in a sieve to drain.

Heat a good splash of oil in a big frying pan. Put 6 small spoonfuls of grated potato beside each other in the pan. Flatten the heaps of potato with the back of the spoon and fry the potato cookies for a few minutes until golden brown and cooked. Put them on kitchen paper to absorb any fat.

Place the potato cookies on two small plates. Divide the egg salad between the cookies and sprinkle with the remaining spring onions and parsley.

Tip: Half the amount of mayonnaise can be replaced by live yogurt or sour cream. Mix thoroughly.

FOR A FAMILY OF FOUR:
DOUBLE THE INGREDIENTS AND SERVE AS A STARTER.

vegetable sticks with a walnut dip

If you want to use this dip as a salad dressing, add a little lemon juice. You could also prepare it with pecan nuts, macadamia nuts or a nut mixture.

6 walnut halves	2 celery stalks
1 tablespoon mayonnaise	⅛ cucumber
1 tablespoon live or soya yogurt	⅛ red pepper
pinch of salt	
pinch of pepper	**2 small portions**

Chop the walnut finely. Add the mayonnaise, the yogurt and the salt and pepper.

Wash the vegetables and deseed the pepper. Cut the vegetables into thin sticks.

Put the walnut dip into small bowls and the vegetable sticks into two small glasses. Put a bowl and a glass of each on two small plates.

FOR A FAMILY OF FOUR:
DOUBLE THE INGREDIENTS AND SERVE AS A SNACK OR A STARTER.

melba toast with smoked salmon and fennel

This is made with raw fennel, which is nice and crispy. If swallowing is difficult, the fennel can be cooked first to soften it. You could also use soft bread instead of toast.

1/4 fennel bulb
1 teaspoon lemon juice
1/2 teaspoon honey
pinch of salt
pinch of pepper
2 tablespoons linseed oil
2 small slices smoked salmon
4 small Melba toasts (preferably wholemeal)
1 tablespoon light cream cheese

2 small portions

Slice the fennel very thinly. Set aside some of the fronds.

Mix the lemon juice with the honey in a big bowl. Stir until the honey is dissolved. Add the salt and pepper, and the oil. Mix well. Add the fennel and let it stand for at least 15 minutes (a few hours would be even better).

Halve the salmon slices. Spread the Melba toasts with cream cheese.

Put on to two small plates. Top with the salmon first and then the fennel salad. Garnish with some fennel fronds.

Tip: Instead of Melba toast, you could also use thinly sliced and toasted wholemeal bread. If dairy products cause problems, you can leave out the cream cheese.

FOR A FAMILY OF FOUR:
THIS WILL BE ENOUGH FOR FOUR PEOPLE TO SERVE AS A SNACK. TO SERVE AS A STARTER, DOUBLE THE INGREDIENTS.

snacks

When buying ready-made snacks, try and go for untreated products without preservatives. Hydrogenated fats can be a problem, especially in crispy snacks, so check the labels first. Recommended ready–to-eat crispy snacks are apples, muesli, radishes and a selection of nuts, but not peanuts.

taco chips with an avocado dip

This dip can also be served as a filling for sandwiches or as a spread on toast. It's nice to add some fresh chives or fresh coriander.

1 small ripe avocado
1 teaspoon of lemon or lime
   juice
1 small tomato
1 spring onion
2 tablespoons sour cream or
   soya yogurt
pinch of salt
pinch of chilli powder
100g taco chips

3–4 small portions

Halve the avocado and take out the stone. Scoop out the flesh and put it in a bowl. Mash lightly with a fork. Add the juice.

Cut the tomato into small pieces and the spring onion into thin rings. Add to the avocado. Fold in the sour cream. Season with a pinch of salt and a pinch of chilli powder.

Fill three or four small bowls, put them on small plates and arrange the taco chips around them.

Tip: If preferred, the tomato can be skinned first. Put it into boiling water for 15 seconds, rinse under cold water and take the skin off with a knife.

FOR A FAMILY OF FOUR:
THIS WILL BE ENOUGH FOR FOUR PEOPLE TO SERVE AS A SNACK. TO SERVE AS A STARTER, DOUBLE THE INGREDIENTS.

caesar salad

It's a good idea to use wholemeal bread for the croutons because it is good for the digestive system. However, if white bread really is preferred, it can also be used. The Parmesan cheese is grated but it could also be shaved into thin slivers.

1 slice wholemeal bread
4 tablespoons olive oil
1 small lemon
2 sprigs of fresh parsley
3 anchovy fillets
1 tablespoon mayonnaise
1 tablespoon live or soya yogurt

2 tablespoons grated Parmesan cheese
pinch of pepper
8–10 small lettuce or Romaine leaves

3–4 small portions

Cut off the crusts and cut the bread into small cubes. Heat the oil and fry the bread cubes for a few minutes until they are crispy. Spoon them on to a piece of kitchen paper.

Wash the lemon and grate the zest. Cut the lemon in half and squeeze out the juice. Chop the parsley very finely. Cut 1 anchovy into long strips.

Pound 2 anchovies to a paste with a pestle and mortar (this can also be done with a fork in a small dish). Add 1 teaspoon of lemon zest, half the parsley, the mayonnaise, the yogurt, half of the cheese and a pinch of pepper. Add lemon juice to taste – about 1/2 or 1 teaspoon.

Wash and dry the lettuce. Divide between two small plates and pour over the anchovy dressing. Put the anchovy strips on top of the salad and then add the croutons, the remaining cheese and remaining parsley.

Tip: For a more pungent taste, add a dash of hot pepper sauce such as Tabasco.

FOR A FAMILY OF FOUR:
2 SLICES OF BREAD AND FRY THEM IN 6 TABLESPOONS OIL. MULTIPLY THE INGREDIENTS FOR THE DRESSING BY FOUR AND USE A WHOLE HEAD OF LETTUCE.

meringues with blueberries and ice cream

Meringues are very sweet and so they are delicious with fresh fruit. You can buy meringue nests or bake them yourself (see tip).

2 small meringue nests
50g blueberries
2 scoops ice cream
1 tablespoon blueberry or
   blackberry syrup

2 small portions

Place the meringue nests on two small plates. Fill them with some of the blueberries and ice cream.

Sprinkle the rest of the blueberries and the syrup over the ice cream.

Tip: If you want to make meringues yourself, here's how to do it. Preheat the oven to 110°C/225°F/gas mark 1/2. Beat 1 egg white with 25g sugar and a pinch of salt until very stiff. Spoon 4 heaps of the mixture on to a baking sheet lined with greaseproof paper. With the back of a spoon, press down the middle of each meringue mixture to form hollow 'nests'. Place in the cool oven and leave them to dry for 2–3 hours.

FOR A FAMILY OF FOUR:
DOUBLE THE INGREDIENTS AND SERVE AS A DESSERT.

everything tastes different

One of the most difficult things to accept during treatment is the fact that tastes can change completely from what you are accustomed to. There is very little to be done about this, other than trying to find out, almost on a daily basis, which tastes suit you best.

green tea granita with honey

Making granita is very easy but it does take time because you have to stir regularly during the freezing process. This prevents it from becoming one big icy lump. You can replace the tea with all sorts of juices, and other sweetened liquids such as coffee or chocolate milk may also be used.

1 tablespoon green tea
$^1/_2$–1 tablespoon honey

2 small portions

Put the green tea in a pot and pour over 250ml of boiling water. Stir in the honey to dissolve. Leave to cool.

Pour the tea into a plastic container and freeze it for 3–4 hours, stirring every 15 minutes.

Divide between two glasses and serve immediately, or seal tightly and keep in the freezer.

FOR A FAMILY OF FOUR:
MULTIPLY THE INGREDIENTS BY THREE AND SERVE AS A DESSERT
OR REFRESHMENT.

strawberry carpaccio

This recipe can be made with any fresh fruit that can be sliced thinly such as melon, peach, pear or mango.

½ tablespoon mixed nuts
½ tablespoon mixed seeds (e.g. sunflower seeds, flaxseeds, sesame seeds, pumpkin seeds)
2 small meringues
10 ripe strawberries
2 teaspoons strawberry syrup
6 tiny fresh mint leaves

2 small portions

FOR A FAMILY OF FOUR:
MULTIPLY THE INGREDIENTS BY
THREE AND SERVE AS A DESSERT.

Chop the nuts coarsely. Roast the nuts and the seeds for a few minutes in a dry frying pan until they start to colour. Slide them on to a plate to cool.

Crumble the meringues.

Wash, hull and thinly slice the strawberries. Overlap the slices, one on top of the other, on two small plates. Sprinkle with the syrup and leave to cool in the fridge for no longer than half a day.

Sprinkle the nuts, seeds, meringue crumbs and mint leaves over the strawberries just before eating.

Tips: Meringues can be ready-bought or home-made. See the instructions for making them on page 130.

lemon curd tarts

These tarts can be filled with the patient's favourite jam or marmalade. The pastry cases can also be baked blind and filled afterwards with fresh fruit and/or whipped cream.

5 tablespoons plain flour
pinch of salt
2 tablespoons sugar
about 25g ice-cold butter
3 tablespoons lemon curd

4 small tarts

Preheat the oven to 180°C/350°F/gas mark 4.

Put the flour and a pinch of salt in a mixing bowl. Add the sugar and rub in the butter until the mixture resembles fine breadcrumbs. This can also be done in a food-processor. Add 1 teaspoon of water. Knead lightly, cover and leave in the fridge for 20 minutes.

Divide the pastry into four small balls and roll each of them out on a floured board into thin rounds about 8cm in diameter. Line four individual, greased, shallow oven or tart dishes with the pastry. Prick some holes in the bottom with a fork. Fill them with the lemon curd. Bake for 15–20 minutes. Cool.

Serve in the dishes.

Tip: Lemon curd can also be home-made. Mix the grated zest of a lemon with 100g honey and 100g butter in a double boiler. Let the butter melt and the honey dissolve. Add the juice of a lemon little by little. Beat 2 eggs and stir slowly into the mixture. Stir until the curd is nice and thick. This may take some time.

FOR A FAMILY OF FOUR:
DOUBLE THE INGREDIENTS AND SERVE WITH COFFEE OR TEA OR AS A DESSERT WITH ICE CREAM ON THE SIDE.

try not to get upset

Eating is an emotional thing, especially when it suddenly becomes a major effort. Try not to get upset if the food you used to like so much does not taste nice at all. It depends on the type of cancer, but for most people, once the chemotherapy has finished, taste returns to normal and you will be able to enjoy your food again.

vegetable tempura with a soy dip

You can make beautiful tempura with big prawns, fish chunks, tender meat and chicken. Just dip them in the batter and fry until golden and cooked. Make sure you use extra virgin olive oil for frying the tempura and don't overheat the oil.

6 small shiitake mushrooms
2 carrots
2 small broccoli florets
⅛ red pepper
50g wholemeal flour
1 egg

pinch of salt
2 tablespoons ground almonds
olive oil
4 tablespoons Japanese soy
   sauce

2–3 small portions

Wipe the shiitake mushrooms, peel the carrots and wash the other vegetables. Cut the carrots into long sticks. Halve the broccoli florets, cut the red pepper into two or three pieces and deseed.

Mix the flour lightly with the egg, 75ml cold water, a pinch of salt and the almonds (a little of the flour may still be seen).

Heat about 4cm of olive oil to 160°C/325°F. You can test the temperature with a cooking thermometer or by frying a piece of bread, which will turn golden in about 1 minute if the oil is at the right temperature.

Fry the tempura in two or three portions. Dip the shiitake mushrooms and vegetables one by one into the batter and put them into the hot oil immediately. Fry for 3–4 minutes until golden brown. Let them dry on a piece of kitchen paper.

Serve on small plates with soy sauce on the side.

Tip: As a variation on a batter made with flour, you could coat the vegetables with beaten egg and wholemeal breadcrumbs.

FOR A FAMILY OF FOUR:
MULTIPLY THE INGREDIENTS BY FOUR AND SERVE AS A STARTER OR SIDE DISH WITH GRILLED FISH OR CHICKEN.

toasted cheese and tomato sandwich

Toasted cheese sandwiches can be made with any cheese that melts easily and all sorts of tasty ingredients can be added, for example, grilled vegetables, chopped nuts and sliced meats without preservatives, such as fresh ham from the butcher or smoked chicken.

2 small tomatoes
small sprig of fresh parsley
2 slices wholemeal bread
1 tablespoon light cream cheese
1 thin slice Cheddar cheese, big
    enough to cover a bread slice
$1/2$ tablespoon olive oil

2 small portions

Wash and then halve the tomatoes. Scoop out the pips and cut the tomatoes into small strips. Chop the parsley finely.

Cut the crusts off the bread. Spread both slices with cream cheese. Divide the tomato strips and the parsley over one slice of bread. Cover with the Cheddar cheese. Put the other slice of bread (cream cheese side down) on top. Press down lightly and brush with a little olive oil.

Heat a big frying pan, put the sandwich in the pan, oil side down, and toast until brown. Brush the top with a little oil, turn and toast until brown. Cut the sandwich into quarters and put them on two small plates.

Tip: Wholemeal bread is recommended but if it causes problems, white bread can be used too. You don't have to use the cream cheese.

FOR A FAMILY OF FOUR:
MULTIPLY THE INGREDIENTS BY FOUR AND SERVE FOR LUNCH.

mild olive oil
During treatment, it's best to avoid very strong tastes, so choose a mild-tasting olive oil.

veal escalopes with a cornflake crust

For extra crispness, these escalopes are coated with cornflakes. Panko Japanese breadcrumbs also give a really crispy result. If a softer texture is preferred, use fresh wholemeal breadcrumbs instead. Be sure to use extra virgin olive oil to deep-fry the chips and make sure that it doesn't overheat.

6 tablespoons organic cornflakes
1 small, thin veal escalope
olive oil
pinch of salt
pinch of pepper
1/2 egg, beaten
1/2 teaspoon paprika
1 teaspoon honey
1/2 tablespoon balsamic vinegar
100g frozen chips
30g mixed salt

2 small portions

Crumble the cornflakes finely.

Cut the escalope into six pieces. Cover them with foil, greased with olive oil. Beat them with a rolling pin to flatten. Season with a pinch of salt, a pinch of pepper and the paprika.

Dip the veal in the egg and cover on both sides with the cornflake crumbs. Leave in the fridge for at least 5 minutes.

Mix the honey with the vinegar and 2 tablespoons of olive oil to make a dressing.

Heat about 10cm of olive oil in a small, deep pan to about 180°C/350°F. Fry the chips until golden brown. Let them dry on kitchen paper. Sprinkle with a little salt.

Heat a splash of olive oil in the meantime and fry the escalopes for a few minutes until brown on both sides.

Dress the salad with the dressing. Divide the salad, the meat and chips between two small plates.

Tip: As a vegetarian alternative to escalopes, you could use slices of aubergine instead. Season the aubergine, cover with cornflakes and fry in the same way as the escalopes.

FOR A FAMILY OF FOUR:
100G CORNFLAKES, 4 VEAL ESCALOPES, 1–2 EGGS, 2 TEASPOONS PAPRIKA, 2 TEASPOONS HONEY, 2 TABLESPOONS BALSAMIC VINEGAR, 8 TABLESPOONS OLIVE OIL FOR THE DRESSING, 1KG FROZEN CHIPS AND PLENTY OF OIL TO DEEP-FRY THEM, 200G MIXED SALAD.

cheese and tomato bread pizza

Instead of sliced bread, you may prefer to use a small amount of pizza dough mix – about 40g should be enough. Roll out the dough very thinly, cover with the sauce and cheese mixture and bake in a very hot oven – not in a pan.

2 large slices wholemeal bread
2 small spring onions
2 cherry tomatoes
1 thick slice mozzarella
$1/2$ teaspoon dried Italian herbs
2 tablespoons olive oil

Cut circles out of the bread slices with a pastry cutter or a cup.

Wash and slice the spring onions thinly. Wash and cut the cherry tomatoes into six wedges and the mozzarella into cubes. Mix the mozzarella with the spring onions, tomatoes and herbs.

Heat the oil in a big frying pan. Fry the bread rounds on a low heat until light brown on one side. Turn and spread the tomato sauce over them. Spoon the mozzarella mixture on top. Half cover the pan. Fry until the other side of the bread is brown and the mozzarella has almost melted.

Serve on two small plates.

Tip: Mozzarella can be replaced by another cheese if you prefer, such as Brie, Camembert or a blue cheese variety.

FOR A FAMILY OF FOUR:
MULTIPLY THE INGREDIENTS BY FOUR AND SERVE AS A STARTER.

spring rolls with chicken and ginger

These can be prepared in advance. Unfried, they will keep in the fridge for 2 days or even longer in the freezer. Serve the spring rolls with a sweet and sour sauce on the side.

about 10cm piece of leek
2 small carrots
about 10g fresh ginger
about 25g smoked or cooked
   chicken
1 garlic clove
1–2 tablespoons olive oil

1/2 tablespoon thick sweet soy
   sauce
1 teaspoon lemon juice
2 thin spring roll sheets (about
   18x18cm)

2 small portions

Preheat the oven to 220°C/425°F/gas mark 7.

Wash the leek. Peel the carrots and ginger. Cut the leek, carrots, ginger and chicken into long, thin strips. Peel and chop the garlic.

Heat 1 tablespoon of olive oil and fry the vegetables and ginger for 4 minutes on a medium heat. Add the chicken, soy sauce and lemon juice and cook for 1 minute more.

Spread out the two spring roll sheets on a worktop and brush them with olive oil.

Divide the vegetable mixture into two portions, putting them at the bottom on top of each spring roll sheet, leaving 3cm free on each side. Fold the sides over the vegetables and roll from the bottom upwards, quite tightly, so you get a small package.

Brush with a little oil and place them on a small baking tray. Bake in the oven for 10–15 minutes until crispy and brown.

Serve them on two small plates.

FOR A FAMILY OF FOUR:
MULTIPLY THE INGREDIENTS BY FOUR AND SERVE AS A STARTER.

cherry crumble

Crumbles are easy to make, even in small portions. Any kind of fruit or fruit compote can also be used.

2 tablespoons wholemeal flour
pinch of salt
1 tablespoon cold butter
1¹/₂ tablespoons icing sugar
pinch of cinnamon
100g cherries (fresh, frozen or
   from a jar)
2 tablespoons cherry jam, preferably
   100% fruit, with no sugar added

2–3 small portions

Preheat the oven to 200°C/400°F/gas mark 6.

Put the flour and a pinch of salt in a mixing bowl. Rub in the butter until the mixture resembles fine breadcrumbs. This can also be done in a food-processor. Stir in the icing sugar and cinnamon and mix well. Keep in the fridge until needed.

Stone the cherries if necessary. Mix the cherries with the jam.

Divide the cherry mixture between two or three greased ramekins or other individual ovenproof dishes. Spoon the crumble over the top.

Bake for about 20 minutes until the crumble is golden and crispy. Serve hot.

Tip: This may be served with whipped cream or ice cream on the side.

FOR A FAMILY OF FOUR:
MULTIPLY THE INGREDIENTS BY FOUR AND SERVE AS A DESSERT.

a preference for sweet or savoury

Most people express a definite preference for either sweet or savoury dishes. During treatment, the idea of a normal menu progression from savoury to sweet no longer applies. The sweet dishes in this book are therefore definitely not meant as desserts, but rather as an alternative to savoury dishes. Two dishes are often simply too much to eat at one sitting.

bread and butter pudding with hazelnuts

This easy-to-prepare pudding can be made with any type of bread and even with cake. It doesn't matter if the slices are a wee bit stale. Instead of using butter, you can sprinkle the bread with a mild olive oil.

1 tablespoon raisins
1 tablespoon unsalted roasted hazelnuts
1½ slices wholemeal bread, cut in half diagonally
1 tablespoon soft butter

1 egg
½–1 tablespoon honey
4 tablespoons whipping or soya cream
½ tablespoon sugar

2 small portions

Soak the raisins for 15 minutes in warm water, drain and leave to dry.

Preheat the oven to 180°C/350°F/gas mark 4.

Chop the hazelnuts coarsely and mix with the raisins. Cut the crusts off and cut each bread slice diagonally in half again to make six triangles. Butter them on both sides.

Beat the egg with the honey and cream until dissolved.

Place a bread triangle at an angle at the bottom of each dish, top with ¼ of the raisin and hazelnut mixture, then with another triangle. Layer with another ¼ of the raisin and hazelnut mixture and finish with a bread triangle. Pour over the egg mixture and soak for 3 minutes.

Sprinkle with sugar and bake in the oven for about 20 minutes until brown and crispy. Serve warm.

Tip: Bread and butter pudding can be served on its own or with whipped cream or custard.

FOR A FAMILY OF FOUR:
MULTIPLY THE INGREDIENTS BY THREE AND SERVE AS A DESSERT.

toasted apple sandwich

This type of sandwich can be toasted in a special iron griddle to be held over the burner of your stove.

¹/₂ apple
4 slices wholemeal bread
¹/₂ tablespoon soft butter
1 teaspoon honey
¹/₂ teaspoon cinnamon

2 small portions

Peel and core the apple half. Cut into very thin slices.

Cut a big round out of each slice of bread using a bowl or pastry cutter. Spread the bread rounds thinly with butter. Cover two with slices of apple and sprinkle with honey and cinnamon. Place the other rounds of bread on top (butter side down) of the others. Press it down a little. Butter the top lightly.

Heat a frying pan. Put the sandwich, butter-side down, in the pan and fry until brown. Butter the top and turn the sandwich to fry on the other side.

Cut the sandwiches in half and serve on two small plates.

Tip: You could replace the apple with banana slices and then you don't have to use butter.

FOR A FAMILY OF FOUR:
MULTIPLY THE INGREDIENTS BY FOUR
AND SERVE AS A SNACK.

orange crème brûlée

The perfect moment to serve the crème brûlée is when the caramel on the top has turned crispy. It is easiest to prepare this sweet a day in advance and then to caramelise the sugar under the grill shortly before serving. As sugar is not really recommended, it is best to eat this sort of dish only on special occasions. You can grill the crème without the sugar. It will turn a lovely brown but it won't be crispy.

1 small orange
8 tablespoons whipping or soya
    cream
1 egg yolk
2 teaspoons custard powder
2 tablespoons honey
about 2 tablespoons caster sugar

2–3 small portions

Wash the orange and grate half over a small saucepan. Halve the orange and squeeze it. Pour the juice into the saucepan. Boil and reduce to 2 tablespoons of juice. Add the cream and bring to a boil.

Beat the egg yolk with the custard powder and the honey for about 5 minutes until light and creamy.

Pour in the hot orange cream in a thin stream, stirring constantly. Pour the mixture back into the saucepan and let it simmer for a few minutes on a very low heat. Keep stirring.

Fill two or three small individual oven dishes with the cream. Let them cool and keep them in the fridge until needed or finish them off.

Preheat a grill or oven to the highest temperature.

Sprinkle the cream with the sugar. Place the dishes under a grill or in the oven and let the sugar caramelise and turn brown.

Tip: If the diameter of the oven dishes is very large, use some more sugar to get an even, crispy layer.

FOR A FAMILY OF FOUR:
MULTIPLY THE INGREDIENTS BY FOUR AND SERVE AS A DESSERT.

too sharp for comfort

Foods that are normally tasty and delicious might not be quite so enjoyable for those who are undergoing treatment. For example, pure orange juice could have a nasty sour and sharp taste. However, you will find out that cooking causes the sharpness to disappear, or you can mix it with honey or banana to soften the taste.

chapter six
firm

creamed chicken sandwich

You may want to warm the bread before making this sandwich. This is easily done in a hot oven – just pop it in for a few minutes.

about 25g cooked chicken
1 small, sweet, pickled gherkin
1 tablespoon mayonnaise
pinch of salt
pinch of pepper
1 small French crusty roll
4 small lettuce leaves
1 tablespoon cranberry sauce

2 small portions

Whizz the chicken, gherkin and 2 tablespoons of the liquid from the gherkin jar to a fine cream in a blender or food processor. Add the mayonnaise and season with a pinch of salt and pepper.

Cut the roll into four long diagonal slices. Spread each slice with a quarter of the creamed chicken. Wash and dry the lettuce leaves and then place a lettuce leaf on each of the slices. Top each with the cranberry sauce.

Serve on two small plates.

FOR A FAMILY OF FOUR:
MULTIPLY THE INGREDIENTS FOR THE CREAM BY FOUR, USE 4 SMALL CRUSTY ROLLS, 16 LETTUCE LEAVES, 2–3 TABLESPOONS OF CRANBERRY SAUCE. SERVE AS A LIGHT LUNCH.

rye bread with cottage cheese and grapes

Rye bread has a coarse texture that can be very pleasant. However, it might not be so appropriate for people who have difficulty swallowing. In this case, replace the rye bread with soft bread, preferably wholemeal.

sprig of fresh parsley
sprig of fresh mint
1 small bunch seedless grapes
2 slices dark rye bread
6 tablespoons cottage cheese

pinch of salt
pinch of pepper
pinch of paprika

2 small portions

Remove the leaves from the stalks of the herbs. Set aside a couple of leaves of each herb and chop the rest finely. Wash and halve the grapes.

Place the slices of rye bread on two small plates. Spoon the cottage cheese on top.

Divide the grapes between the two cottage cheese-covered pieces of bread. Sprinkle with a pinch of salt, a pinch of pepper and paprika and the herbs. Place the reserved herb leaves on top.

Tip: As an alternative to grapes, strawberries or slices of apple may be used.

FOR A FAMILY OF FOUR:
DOUBLE THE INGREDIENTS AND SERVE AS A SNACK.

grilled vegetable and mozzarella salad

With its soft and sweetish taste, balsamic vinegar should appeal to patients. However, for some people it might still taste acidic, in which case, mix it with some honey.

sprig of fresh basil
1/8 yellow pepper
1/4 courgette
1/4 fennel bulb
3 cherry tomatoes
1/2 tablespoon olive oil
pinch of salt
pinch of pepper
1/2 tablespoon balsamic vinegar
1/2 ball of mozzarella or 3 mini balls
6 small lettuce leaves

2 small portions

Remove the basil leaves from the stem and reserve to garnish. Finely chop the stem.

Wash the vegetables. Cut the pepper in half and deseed. Slice the courgette and fennel. Halve the cherry tomatoes. Brush each of the vegetables with a little olive oil and grill them for a few minutes on each side.

Sprinkle the warm vegetables with 1/2 tablespoon of olive oil, a pinch each of salt and pepper, the basil stems and 1/4 tablespoon of balsamic vinegar. Set aside to cool.

Cut the mozzarella into wedges. Wash and dry the lettuce leaves and arrange them on two small plates. Scatter over the grilled vegetables, mozzarella wedges and basil leaves.

Tip: The mozzarella can be replaced by a stronger tasting cheese, like Gorgonzola.

FOR A FAMILY OF FOUR:
MULTIPLY THE INGREDIENTS BY FOUR AND SERVE AS A STARTER.

bigger portions

For most patients, small portions work best during treatment. However, should a patient ask for more, you can easily just prepare bigger portions.

apple, celery and brazil nut quiche

Quiches like this are great to have on hand. Properly covered and kept in the fridge, they will last for about 3 days. They may also be served warm. If you wish, you can make this without cheese.

2 eggs
4 tablespoons flour
pinch of salt
2 tablespoons cold butter
1 small celery stick
1 spring onion
2 brazil nuts

1 small, thin bacon rasher
1 tablespoon olive oil
pinch of pepper
2 tablespoons grated Cheddar
   cheese

2 small portions

Separate one of the eggs. Beat the yolk.

Put the flour and a pinch of salt in a mixing bowl and rub in the butter until the mixture resembles fine breadcrumbs. This can also be done in a food-processor. Stir in 1 tablespoon of the beaten egg yolk and 1 teaspoon of cold water. Knead lightly, cover and chill in the fridge for 20 minutes.

Preheat the oven to 180°C/350°F/gas mark 4.

Wash the celery and spring onion and chop finely. Chop the brazil nuts finely. Slice the bacon finely.

Heat the oil in a pan and fry the bacon with the celery for 5 minutes. Add the spring onion and fry for 2 minutes. Stir in the nuts.

Add the egg white and the other whole egg to the rest of the yolk. Beat well and season.

Divide the pastry into two small balls and roll them out on a floured surface to 10cm rounds. Line two small oven dishes with the pastry. Prick the pastry with a fork. Fill the dishes with the celery mixture, sprinkle with the cheese and pour in the eggs.

Bake for 20–25 minutes in the oven. Set aside to cool.

Tip: Brazil nuts contain vitamin E and enhance the effects of selenium (an antioxidant).

FOR A FAMILY OF FOUR:
DOUBLE THE INGREDIENTS AND SERVE AS A STARTER.

sweet and sour prawns

This also tastes good with a few tablespoons of pineapple or mango pieces. Stir them in with the spring onions.

10 tablespoons easy-cook
  whole grain rice
2 small broccoli florets
2 spring onions
1 garlic clove
2 raw king prawns
1 tablespoon olive oil

1–2 teaspoons lime juice
4 tablespoons tomato ketchup
1 teaspoon thick sweet soy
  sauce

2 small portions

Cook the rice in boiling water following the instructions on the packet. Drain.

Wash the broccoli and spring onions. Cut the broccoli into very small florets. Slice the spring onions. Peel and chop the garlic.

Peel the prawns but leave the tails on. Cut them lengthwise in the direction of the tail but not quite through. Take out the black/brown intestine.

Heat the oil in a wok or frying pan and stir-fry the broccoli for 3 minutes. Add the prawns and stir-fry for another 3 minutes. Add the spring onions and garlic and, after 1 minute, stir in the lime juice to taste, the tomato ketchup and soy sauce.

Divide the rice and sweet and sour prawns between two small plates. Serve cold or warm.

Tip: You can also add some hot pepper sauce such as Tabasco for a bit of pep.

FOR A FAMILY OF FOUR:
350G EASY-COOK WHOLE GRAIN RICE, 600G BROCCOLI, A LARGE BUNCH OF SPRING ONIONS, 3 GARLIC CLOVES, 500G RAW PRAWNS, A SPLASH OF OLIVE OIL, THE JUICE OF 1 SMALL LIME, 150ML KETCHUP, 1–2 TABLESPOONS OF THICK SWEET SOY SAUCE. SERVE AS A MAIN COURSE.

individual apple pies

Apple is a much-loved fruit and readily available. It also works well with other ingredients such as nuts, raisins and currants, which can be added according to taste.

5 tablespoons wholemeal flour
pinch of salt
2 tablespoons sugar
2½ tablespoons ice-cold butter
1 small lemon
1 small apple or ½ apple
1 teaspoon honey
½ teaspoon cinnamon
1 tablespoon skimmed or soya milk

2 small pies

Put the flour and a pinch of salt in a mixing bowl, add the sugar and rub in the butter until the mixture resembles fine breadcrumbs. This can also be done in a food-processor. Add 1 teaspoon of water. Knead lightly, cover and chill in the fridge for 20 minutes.

Preheat the oven to 180°C/350°F/gas mark 4.

Wash the lemon and grate a quarter of the zest. Squeeze out the lemon juice. Peel and core the apple. Cut into wedges and then cut the wedges into slices. Mix them with the lemon zest, 2 teaspoons of lemon juice, the honey and cinnamon.

Divide the pastry into four small balls and roll each of them out on a floured surface into thin 8cm rounds. Line two individual oven or tart dishes with two rounds of the pastry. Prick the pastry with a fork and fill the dishes with the apple slices.

Cover the apple filing with the remaining pastry rounds and crimp the two layers together with a thumb and index finger. Make a hole in the middle.

Bake for 20–25 minutes in the hot oven. Brush the top with some milk and bake for a further few minutes. Set aside to cool.

Tip: Brushing the tops of the apple pies with a few drops of milk gives a nice shine to the pastry. You could also use beaten egg, which should be brushed on before the pies are put into the oven.

snacks

Some good ready-to-eat firm snacks are quiches, mini pizzas, pears and pineapple. Try and stay away from E numbers and hydrogenated fats – always check the labels.

FOR A FAMILY OF FOUR:
DOUBLE THE INGREDIENTS AND SERVE AS A SNACK WITH A CUP OF COFFEE OR TEA, OR WITH ICE CREAM AS A DESSERT.

apricot and pine nut yogurt roll

Fresh apricots are very good in this recipe but, as they are not always available, dried fruit is used. If you use fresh apricots, halve them, take out the stone, chop and mix them into the dough.

5 tablespoons live or soya
 yogurt
1 small tablespoon olive oil
5 tablespoons wholemeal flour
pinch of salt
2 tablespoons honey

4 tablespoons pine nuts
6 ready-to-eat dried apricots
1/2 teaspoon icing sugar

2–3 small portions

Mix the yogurt with the olive oil, flour, salt and 1 tablespoon of honey. Work it quickly to a soft dough. Put it in the fridge to rest for 20 minutes.

Roast the pine nuts in a dry frying pan until light brown and set them aside to cool on a plate.

Preheat the oven to 180°C/350°F/gas mark 4.

Cut the apricots into small pieces.

Roll out the dough on a floured surface into a thick 12 x 12cm square. Sprinkle the apricots and pine nuts on top and push into the dough. Drizzle over the rest of the honey.

Roll up the dough and cut it into six slices. Line a baking tray with baking parchment and bake the slices on it for about 30 minutes until golden brown. Set aside to cool.

Place the rolls on two or three small plates and dust with icing sugar.

Tip: The pine nuts can be replaced by macadamia, pecan or cashew nuts, all chopped coarsely.

FOR A FAMILY OF FOUR:
DOUBLE THE INGREDIENTS AND SERVE WITH A CUP OF COFFEE OR TEA.

fresh fruit ice lollies

These frozen ice lollies can be made with all sorts of individual or mixed soft fruits. Hard fruits like apples and pears can also be used but have to be cooked first in a small pan with a few spoonfuls of water until soft. The ice lollies can be kept in the freezer for weeks.

250g mixed strawberries,
   raspberries and cherries
2–4 tablespoons honey
1 tablespoon lemon juice

serves 3–6

Wash the strawberries, raspberries and cherries. Stone the cherries.

Whizz all the fruit in a blender or food-processor with honey to taste and the lemon juice.

Fill 3–6 lollipop moulds with the fruit mixture so they are three quarters full. Place the sticks in the moulds and leave to freeze in the freezer for a few hours.

Take the fresh fruit ice lollies out of the moulds just before you are going to eat them.

Tip: The size and number of the ice lollies depends on the size of the ice moulds.

FOR A FAMILY OF FOUR:
THE RECIPE IS ENOUGH FOR A FAMILY IF YOU ARE USING SMALL MOULDS. IF THE FRUIT MIXTURE DOESN'T FILL ENOUGH MOULDS, DOUBLE THE INGREDIENTS.

nougat pot cakes

These cakes are easy to make and can be filled with all sorts of tasty ingredients like caramel toffees, nuts, pieces of chocolate and berries. In this recipe, nougat and dried fruits are used as the filling.

3 pieces (about 30g) soft nougat
1 piece (about 25g) dried mango or
   2 dried apricots
5 tablespoons wholemeal flour
1 teaspoon baking powder
pinch of salt
3 tablespoons butter
3 tablespoons beaten egg
2½ tablespoons runny honey
about 50ml skimmed or soya milk

serves 3–4

Preheat the oven to 220°C/425°F/gas mark 7.

Cut the nougat and dried mango or apricots into small pieces.

Mix the flour with the baking powder and a pinch of salt. Add the nougat, mango and apricot pieces.

Melt the butter. Mix the egg with the honey and the milk and stir into the butter. Beat the milk mixture quickly into the flour mixture.

Fill three or four small greased ramekins with the batter. Bake in the oven for 10 minutes, then turn down the heat down to 180°C/350°F/gas mark 4. Bake for a further 5–10 minutes until golden brown. Leave to cool and serve in the ramekins.

Tip: Honey can be used instead of sugar as it is thought to be healthier than sugar. However, it won't give the cakes as good a texture.

FOR A FAMILY OF FOUR:
DOUBLE THE INGREDIENTS AND SERVE WITH A CUP OF COFFEE OR TEA.

problems with dairy

If eating or drinking dairy products results in heightened mucus production, you'd better choose savoury dishes using dairy products as the salt in savoury foods has a clearing effect on the mucus.

grilled chicken with fried potatoes

These chicken skewers are also good served with a small portion of apple or cranberry sauce.

1 small red onion
2 sprigs of fresh mint
2 small potatoes
80g chicken breast
1½ tablespoons olive oil

pinch of salt
pinch of pepper
6 tablespoons fresh or frozen
 peas

Peel the onion and cut into four wedges. Halve these and take the layers of onion apart. Remove the leaves from the sprigs of mint. Leave the small leaves whole and halve the bigger ones. Peel the potatoes and slice thinly.

Cut the chicken into 12 small cubes. Mix them with 1 teaspoon of olive oil and a pinch each of salt and pepper.

Skewer pieces of chicken, onion and mint leaves on to six small skewers. Chop the rest of the onion and mint finely.

Cook the peas in boiling water until quite soft. Drain and mix with the chopped mint.

Heat 1 tablespoon of oil in a frying pan. Put the potato slices side by side in the pan and fry them until golden brown on both sides, turning them every so often. Add the chopped onion and fry lightly.

Grill the chicken skewers in a hot grill pan or under the grill until brown and well done.

Arrange the potatoes, peas and skewers on two small plates.

Tip: The chicken skewers (prepared but uncooked) can be kept in the fridge for a day.

FOR A FAMILY OF FOUR:
3 SMALL RED ONIONS, A SMALL BUNCH OF FRESH MINT, 1KG POTATOES, 300G CHICKEN, 4 TABLESPOONS OLIVE OIL, 600G PEAS.

baked potatoes with spinach cream and ham

The baked potatoes are cut open and slightly scruffed up before serving and the cream is put on top. If a finer texture is preferred, the potato flesh can be scooped out, puréed with the spinach cream and then spooned back into the skin for an appetising look.

2 small baking potatoes
pinch of salt
1 thin slice fresh ham without
    preservatives, from the butcher
1 small onion
100g spinach

1/2 tablespoon olive oil
2 tablespoons crème fraîche or
    soya yogurt
pinch of pepper

2 small portions

Preheat the oven to 220°C/425°F/gas mark 7.

Scrub the potatoes under the tap and place each on a piece of foil. Sprinkle with the salt and fold the foil tightly around the potatoes. Put them on a baking tray and bake for about 1 hour until done.

Cut the ham into small ribbons. Peel and chop the onion. Wash and dry the spinach, then chop it.

Heat the oil in a frying pan and fry the onion for 3 minutes on a low heat. Turn the heat up, add the spinach and stir-fry for 4 minutes. Strain the mixture until most of the liquid has been removed.

Mix in the ham and the crème fraîche just before serving. Season with a pinch of salt and pepper and heat for a few minutes.

Take the potatoes out of the oven. Unfold the foil, cut the potatoes open and criss-cross the potato surface with a fork.

Put the potatoes on two small plates and spoon in the spinach cream.

Tip: You can also use frozen spinach or replace it with watercress, rocket or peas.

FOR A FAMILY OF FOUR:
DOUBLE THE INGREDIENTS AND SERVE AS A STARTER OR SIDE DISH.

baked tortillas

These tortillas can be prepared in advance and kept in the fridge until needed. Heat them up in the oven just before serving. You don't have to use the cheese.

1/4 red pepper
sprig of fresh coriander
1 tablespoon olive oil
50g minced beef or chicken
1/2 teaspoon Mexican or taco spices
2 tablespoons cooked tinned kidney
  beans
2 tablespoons tinned sweetcorn
5 tablespoons tomato ketchup or pasta
  sauce
1 small soft tortilla
4 tablespoons grated Cheddar cheese
2 tablespoons sour cream or soya
  yogurt

2 small portions

Preheat the oven to 200°C/400°F/gas mark 6.

Wash, deseed and chop the red pepper. Chop the coriander.

Heat the olive oil in a big frying pan or wok. Stir-fry the beef or chicken for 3 minutes. Add the red pepper and stir-fry for another 3 minutes. Stir in the spices, beans, sweetcorn and tomato ketchup or sauce. Simmer for 2 minutes.

Cut the tortilla in half. Fold in the sides to form a cone and put them in one or two small oven dishes, folded side underneath. Spoon in the bean mixture. Sprinkle the tortillas with cheese and cover with foil.

Bake for 5 minutes in the oven until nice and warm and the cheese has melted.

Sprinkle with the coriander and serve in the dish or on small plates. Add sour cream to taste.

Tip: If it is difficult to get minced chicken, chop chicken meat finely with a sharp knife or pulse in a food-processor.

FOR A FAMILY OF FOUR:
2 RED PEPPERS, 6 SPRIGS OF FRESH CORIANDER, 3 TABLESPOONS OLIVE OIL, 200G MINCED BEEF OR CHICKEN, 2 TEASPOONS MEXICAN OR TACO SPICES, 1 X 400G TIN KIDNEY BEANS, 1 LARGE TIN SWEETCORN, 250ML TOMATO KETCHUP OR SAUCE, 7–8 SMALL SOFT TORTILLAS, 150G GRATED CHEDDAR CHEESE, 200ML SOUR CREAM.

the smell of food
For patients, the smell of food often causes nausea, so naturally it's best to choose ingredients without a strong smell. Ideally, try to prepare food when the patient is not around. You may even consider using your neighbours' kitchen. In almost all cases, it is easier for patients not to have to cook for themselves.

curried veal stew with pasta

1 small onion
125g lean stewing veal
pinch of salt
pinch of pepper
1 tablespoon olive oil
½ tablespoon mild curry
    powder
50ml sweet white wine

200ml veal stock
2 small nests pappardelle
about 50g fresh or frozen
    peas
2 tablespoons crème fraîche
    or soya cream

2–3 small portions

Peel and chop the onion. Cut the meat into small cubes of about 1.5cm and season with the salt and pepper.

Heat the oil in a small frying pan and sauté the meat cubes on a medium heat for a few minutes until brown. Add the onion, sprinkle with the curry powder and fry for two minutes. Add the wine and the stock. Bring to the boil and then turn down to the very lowest heat. Cover and stew for 1 hour until the meat is soft.

Cook the pappardelle in boiling water with a pinch of salt for 2 minutes longer than the instructions on the packet. Add the peas 8 minutes before the end of the cooking time. Strain.

Add the crème fraîche or cream to the stew, stir a little and let it simmer for a few minutes longer. Season.

Divide the pasta and stew between two or three small plates or bowls.

Tip: You can use apple juice instead of wine.

FOR A FAMILY OF FOUR:
MULTIPLY THE INGREDIENTS BY THREE BUT USE 350G PAPPARDELLE AND 600G PEAS.

mini meatballs in fresh tomato sauce

Although this recipe uses fresh tomato sauce, you can use ready-made tomato sauce to make life a little easier.

2 potatoes
salt and pepper
sprig of fresh basil
1/4 slice wholemeal bread
50g finely minced veal or beef
1 1/2 tablespoons beaten egg
1 tablespoon olive oil
2 celery sticks
1 small onion
2 tomatoes

2 small portions

Peel the potatoes and cut them into pieces. Cook in a small pan with a little water and a pinch of salt for 15–20 minutes until they are done. Drain.

Take the leaves off the basil and reserve for garnishing. Chop the stem finely.

Whizz the bread with half of the chopped basil stems in a blender or food-processor to make breadcrumbs. Mix the minced meat with half of the breadcrumb mixture, a pinch each of salt and pepper and 1 tablespoon of the beaten egg. Divide into six portions and roll them into balls.

Heat 1/2 tablespoon of oil in a small frying pan and fry the meatballs for about 10 minutes until brown.

Wash the celery sticks. Cut half of one finely into very small pieces. Slice the rest into thin strips. Put the celery strips in a pan of slightly salted boiling water and cook for about 10 minutes. Drain.

Peel and chop the onion. Wash the tomatoes and chop.

Heat 1/2 tablespoon of oil in a frying pan. Add the onion, finely cut celery and remaining basil stems. Fry for 3 minutes on a medium heat. Add the tomatoes, a pinch each of salt and pepper and fry for 2 more minutes. Add 5 tablespoons of water, the rest of the bread mixture and the meatballs. Let the sauce simmer for 5 minutes. Adjust the seasoning.

Mash the potatoes in the pan. Put them back on the heat and stir in the rest of the egg. Heat for a few minutes and add salt and pepper to taste.

Divide the mash, celery and mini meatballs with sauce between two small plates. Tear the basil leaves and scatter them over the top.

Tip: Celery works well as an ingredient in the sauce but it's also good as a side dish. It can be replaced by fennel if you wish.

FOR A FAMILY OF FOUR:
1KG POTATOES, 1 SLICE WHOLEMEAL BREAD, 3 SPRIGS OF FRESH BASIL, 300G MINCED MEAT, 1 EGG, 1 HEAD OF CELERY, 2 ONIONS, 4 TOMATOES, 3–4 TABLESPOONS OLIVE OIL. USE THREE QUARTERS OF THE EGG FOR THE MEATBALLS AND THE REST FOR THE MASH. USE 1 CELERY STICK FOR THE SAUCE.

fried pineapple

Fresh or tinned pineapple can be used in this recipe. Since tinned pineapple has already been sweetened, no honey is needed.

1/2 tablespoon shelled sunflower
    seeds
1 slice fresh or tinned pineapple
a small knob of butter or a splash
    of olive oil
1/2 tablespoon honey (optional)
2 scoops vanilla ice cream

2 small portions

Roast the sunflower seeds for a few minutes in a dry frying pan over a high heat, stirring all the time. Set aside to cool on a plate.

Cut the pineapple horizontally into two thin slices.

Melt the butter in a frying pan and fry the pineapple for 2 minutes on each side over a medium heat. When fresh pineapple is used, add the honey and let it melt.

Place the pineapple on two small plates. Put a scoop of ice cream in the middle and sprinkle with the sunflower seeds.

Tip: Slices of peeled apple can be prepared in more or less the same way as the pineapple.

FOR A FAMILY OF FOUR:
MULTIPLY THE INGREDIENTS BY FOUR AND SERVE AS A DESSERT.

peanuts are off the menu
Seeds are very good for you and most nuts too. When using mixed nuts in recipes, choose a selection without peanuts as peanuts aren't recommended for cancer patients.

apple fritters

Fritters often go down well. Try also using bananas, apricots and pineapple. However the fruit you choose shouldn't be too juicy (this would make the fritters soggy) and it should have a firm texture.

1 apple
1 tablespoon blanched
   almonds
25g wholemeal flour
1/2 beaten egg
pinch of salt

mild olive oil
2 scoops apple or lemon sorbet
1 teaspoon icing sugar

2 small portions

Peel and core the apples. Cut into six wedges. Chop the almonds coarsely.

Mix the flour lightly with the egg, 75ml cold water, a pinch of salt and the almonds.

Heat about 4cm of olive oil in a saucepan to 160°C/325°F. You can test the temperature with a cooking thermometer or by frying a piece of bread, which will turn golden in about 1 minute if the oil is at the right temperature.

Dip the apple wedges one by one into the batter and immediately put them into the hot oil. Fry for 3–4 minutes until golden brown. Remove from the oil and dry on a piece of kitchen paper.

Place the scoops of apple or lemon sorbet on two or three small plates. Place the fritters next to them and dust with icing sugar.

Tip: Apple sorbet is not always easy to find. It can be replaced by any other type of sorbet or ordinary ice cream.

FOR A FAMILY OF FOUR:
MULTIPLY THE INGREDIENTS BY FOUR AND SERVE AS A DESSERT.

rice pudding

200ml skimmed or soya milk
5 tablespoons whipping or
   soya cream
2 tablespoons easy-cook
   dessert rice
1/2–1 tablespoon honey
3 tablespoons thick berry juice
2 stems of redcurrants
   (optional)

2 small portions

FOR A FAMILY OF FOUR:
MULTIPLY THE INGREDIENTS BY
FOUR AND SERVE AS A DESSERT.

This rice pudding is also nice when served cold. It will get thicker when it cools down and may be made smoother by adding a little more milk or cream. Hot or cold, it tastes good with a tablespoon of chopped nuts.

Bring the milk, cream, rice and honey to a boil in a small saucepan. Turn down the heat as low as possible and let the mixture simmer until the rice is soft and creamy, stirring every now and then (the cooking time varies per brand and will be stated on the packet).

Divide between two small bowls. Pour over the berry juice and serve hot. Put the washed redcurrants on the side if using.

Tip: If berry juice is not available, 100% fruit jam can be used.

french toast with red fruit

French toast can also be served with fruit salad made from seasonal fruit.

4 tablespoons mixed fresh or
   frozen red fruit such as
   berries and cherries
1 teaspoon honey
1 egg
1½ teaspoons vanilla sugar
pinch of salt
1 slice light wholemeal bread
a small knob of butter or a
   splash of olive oil

2 small portions

Clean the fruit or let it defrost. Mix the fruit with the honey.

Whisk the egg with 1 teaspoon of the vanilla sugar and the salt until the sugar has dissolved.

Cut the slice of bread diagonally into four pieces.

Melt the butter or heat the oil in a small frying pan. Dip the pieces of bread deep into the egg mixture and fry them until brown on both sides.

Place the French toast on two small plates. Spoon the fruit over and dust with the remaining vanilla sugar.

Tip: French toast is usually sweet but it can also be savoury. No sugar is used and chopped fresh herbs and pepper are added to the egg mix. When almost done, grated cheese that melts easily can be sprinkled on top.

FOR A FAMILY OF FOUR:
MULTIPLY THE INGREDIENTS BY FOUR BUT USE ONLY 2 EGGS. SERVE AS A BREAKFAST TREAT.

sharing meals
Patients often find it easier to eat with some company but be aware that they can easily lose their appetite when they see the size of normal portions on other plates.

index